T0128037

Heaven On Earth Begins

The Seven Stages of Love

TALA SCOTT

BALBOA.
PRESS

A DIVISION OF HAY HOUSE

Balboa Press books may be ordered through booksellers or by contacting:

Balboa Press
A Division of Hay House
1663 Liberty Drive
Bloomington, IN 47403
www.balboapress.com.au
1 (877) 407-4847

Print information available on the last page.

ISBN: 978-1-5043-1385-8 (sc)
ISBN: 978-1-5043-1386-5 (e)

Balboa Press rev. date: 09/06/2018

Dedication

To Christine
My loving sister and beautiful friend

And to those who believe in love

Contents

Preface

Heaven on Earth Begins. The next level of teaching is ready to commence. My first book, *Heaven on Earth*, provided a glimpse into a new world concerning love and relationships. Wisdom and knowledge accumulates within the sacred heart as it prepares to traverse the intricate road ahead. The clearing away of limiting patterns and beliefs must be completed now. It is time to get serious if you want the Divine Union Relationship.

The teaching contained in this book is referred to as the 'Seven Stages of Love'. Innovative ideas pave the way forward to the most amazing relationship we will ever know. We ask relevant questions that need to be answered. What is love? How do we obtain it? How do we keep it forever? We are all seeking answers and searching for truth.

Our world has evolved during the past decade. But our deepest need to love and be loved has not. It is time to experience and embrace a brave new world as we cultivate self-love and inner strength. We have been told that our bravery will be rewarded. It's important to remember that the power of positive thinking can bring to fruition the extraordinary lives we are meant to live.

The family of humanity is ready to move forward and take the next evolutionary steps toward an inspired life. Just like the lotus flower pushes through the water's surface to bloom, the heart pushes its way forward toward the soft stirrings of divine love.

The Divine Union Relationship is linked to love, integrity, beauty and truth. The true meaning of miracles is found within the mysteries of the sacred heart that have stood the test of time. We are being encouraged to enter the next level of new experiences as they are revealed. These new experiences leave clues, a treasure map of scattered gems, as new pathways appear encouraging us to explore love more freely and deeply than ever before.

The sacred heart knows the way. The map is alight with anticipation Are you ready?

Introduction

A decade has passed since I wrote my first book *Heaven on Earth*. Numerous life experiences swirl within my heart. Anticipation fills me to the brim as I sit at my desk to transcribe the next level of the Divine Union Relationship.

Only the brave in heart, body, soul and mind can fully understand the wonderment of this new love story that is beginning to emerge. My soul dances in connection to the rhythm of new and amazing life situations and circumstances. The information I have discovered takes the Divine Union Relationship forward in a positive and expansive direction.

It's my belief that we are emerging from the dark cocoon of the unknown veils of illusion that blind us and bind us to the harsh world of pain and suffering. Some people endure so much suffering that they want to give up on life, they don't want to go on. New truths are beginning to emerge that in time will set us free. However, as we begin, there are steps to take and obstacles to overcome.

The wisdom I have obtained during the past ten years has revealed that the path to secure freedom comes at a price. It demands our willingness to let go of life's struggles and to cultivate the understanding that we deserve so much more. In truth, I was faced with the demands of change and growth, to remove outdated patterns and limiting belief systems. The suffering we endure from this state of awareness creates emotional and mental wounds. It leaves us exhausted, exposed, fragile and broken. Endurance of pain can result in an armour like shell that surrounds and tightly squeezes the sacredness and sanctity of the heart. The ability to truly shine and live to our full potential is lost, as fear has immobilised us. To love and be loved is the true key required to unlock the heart's hidden treasures.

The road I have travelled and the experiences I have shared with the men portrayed in the Seven Stages of Love opened my life to higher truths and understanding of the human heart, body, soul and mind. I have known first-hand happiness, joy and wonderment as I discovered deep emotions regarding the synergy of love. Rejection, pain and releasing old emotional wounds also surfaced as I learnt about the limitations that kept me isolated and alone. There was much work to do. Ultimately, the journey has led me to the discovery of my authentic self, to inner peace, joy and the understanding that I can now access the purest love contained in the Divine Union Relationship.

I am convinced that we were not born to suffer. It's my belief that we are born to experience all possibilities and especially, the best that life has to offer. We must let the balance of the heart and mind guide our lives as we evolve and bond together as the family of humanity. The Divine Union Relationship holds the keys we seek. We can and should have it all!

Now that I have completed and integrated the seven stages of love into my heart, I am ready to soar to new horizons. As I reflect, I acknowledge that I am not the same woman I once was. Gentleness, love, gratitude and a deepening sense of compassion and joy now fills my heart. I am brave, compassionate and open to experience the new life opportunities that await me. As a young woman, I possessed enormous faith and courage, yet I continually stumbled through life. This occurred, because like most people, I had limited knowledge of the core teachings of love and relationships.

Education and healing are our best courses of action and the most progressive steps we can take toward achieving our goals. It is my purpose and honour to teach the Divine Union Relationship, to point the way out of the maze of confusion and limited understanding. The place to start this inner and outer journey of transformation begins with ourselves. The basis of our happiness and joy depends on it! Honouring and loving yourself illuminates the map that leads to the ultimate destination. It is the cornerstone and fabric of the future we can build together.

Prologue

Starry, starry night

The silky eminence of the universe shimmers with light. I can feel the intensity of vibration beginning to emerge from a source, as yet, unknown. In this moment, I am unaware that a star is preparing to explode. The vibration escalates and the rumbling amplifies as I watch, enraptured, the scene unfolding around me.

I am awake in a dream-vision experience once again and consciously aware of all that is happening. I am witnessing miraculous phenomena. I smile with absolute delight. My body is floating in the luminous dark mass of space. Feelings of immense love are pulsating toward me. Stars, too numerous to count, are twinkling and tumbling like precious jewels, bewilderingly beautiful. All I feel is a deep, abiding love and connection to my beloved stars.

Our universe is breathtaking and vast, absolutely beyond measure. Dust particles swirl past, dancing and swaying and tumbling in their cosmic playground. Majestic hues of colour and light swirl with effortless grace. As my eyes search the endless void of space, I see light fragments swirl and intertwine with radiating nebulae. It can only be described as perfection at play. I am completely overwhelmed by all that I see.

My heart is thumping extraordinarily fast. Prisms of light shimmer and glow silhouetted against the pitch-black void. It is not death I am about to witness, but the birth of life anew. The birth of the supernova is immanent!

Flickering energy involutes, dancing and swaying to the rhythm of atomic particles preparing to reach a critical mass. I hear a rumbling so deafening it defies description. As the inevitable outcome approaches, the reverberation within the impending explosion is unbelievably intense. At this stage I feel no fear. I am floating like a soft, white feather hovering in the magnificence of star-filled space as I am reverently, tenderly held within the vibrating arms of the universe.

Fear quietly seeps into my mind like gentle rain falling. A realisation dawns! A star is going to explode and I'm floating in the universe with it! "What am I going to do?" I ask myself. "Oh no, I'm going to die." Panic rises within me and my pulse pounds in my ears like thunderous tribal drums. Conscious thought interrupts my state of panic and I remind myself to breathe. "Be brave, just breathe," I tell myself out loud. Any moment now, death will come for me.

In a split second, as if orchestrated by an invisible force, all thoughts cease. An all-pervading stillness ensues. Love permeates my heart and the chatter in my mind fades away. An almighty explosion is heard. The blast expands within the invisible force of nature. I cover my eyes from the shock waves and the colour blinding my eyes. Creation, however, hovers in the simplicity and complexity of its grandeur. The symphony of the universe is singing a song more beautiful than before.

Renewed energy, light and brilliance has formed from the star's death. Bewildered and in shock, I watch, and then stand in awe at the birth of this majestic supernova. An epiphany dawns, a deeper understanding suddenly emerges. My beloved star is gone, obliterated with the finality that accompanies death. The heightened energy of the new star is just beginning to evolve, exuding secrets that are yet to be discovered.

"What just happened?" I ask myself in disbelief. My reasoning mind tells me I should be dead, but I am still very much alive! There is a part of us that never dies. We change, transform and become more incredible than ever before. There is no death! We are immortal.

My eyes shine with clarity and wonderment at the brilliance of creation. My heart is exploding in cosmic bliss. Intense pulsations of love wash over me connecting me to the link, the heart of humankind. A remembrance stirs, an absolute knowing is now revealing that a greater plan has emerged.

The dream-vision slowly shimmers and is gone.

I woke with a shudder and bolted upright in my bed. It was January 1, 2015. My mind was having difficulty comprehending all that I had witnessed. The feeling of absolute love and wonderment toward creation came flooding back with intensity and awe. I had just witnessed the birth of a supernova and the significance of the miracle was crystal clear. My life was going to change dramatically.

Rainbow coloured birds were playing outside my bedroom window, chirping loudly with animated delight. I adore birds, yet

I was wishing that they would chirp with a little less enthusiasm. I wasn't quite ready to embrace the day. I also loved my new bed and especially my luxurious Vera Wang doona and 1,000 thread count cotton sheets. Ah, the bliss! More importantly, I wanted to hold onto this sacred feeling for as long as humanly possible. I know I am incredibly lucky to witness and remember my dream-vision explorations.

This New Year held amazing life experiences that were preparing to unfold. It contained the secret of magical events that were going to herald the new direction my life would take. It also contained the joy of transcribing all the experiences that needed to be included in this book.

The seven stages of love are ready to begin.

The First Stage of Love
Karmic Contract – Mr Grey

This book you now hold in your hands
Contains the secret of love's commands
The Divine Union Relationship is real and bold
The Seven Stages of Love can now be told
Love is the key the heart searches for
Found in the inner sanctum, the heart's true core
Read the words of love divine
They're real, true and so sublime
The heart really does know what to do
Follow this map, the real-life clues
If not, you'll fall into a daze
And walk into the relationship maze
Challenges appear, there's no more fun
The clues are gone; a whirlwind has spun
Until you know what love is not
You will tie your heart in knots

Until you decide to follow the clues
The Divine Union Relationship won't flow to you
Heal the heart of old wounds and pain
That's how to free the heart again
Rejection and hurt, those deep old wounds
Need to be healed and then the heart swoons
Remember what I say is true
Divine love will reveal its path to you
Read this book with an open heart
Then true wisdom begins to spark
And reveals the real, the inner you
This opens the doorway to the first stage clue

Chapter 1

Childhood Dreams

A strong gusting southerly wind whipped and whistled through ancient trees anchored on a seven-acre property nestled in a country township in Australia. A little boy, aged five, stood on the back porch of his family home. He was dressed like an urchin with dirt smeared across his face and shirt. Yet, this little boy was strong, he possessed the heart of a true warrior.

His destiny was whispered in haunting tones that arose within the symphony of the whistling wind. But he didn't hear the melody, the symphony's call. His mind was preoccupied with other things. A small container of food and water was added to his backpack. The food and water contained the nourishment he needed for his body but not for his soul. The little warrior slipped into his sneakers and stepped off the porch to begin his daily trek.

Tiny fingers gently brushed over tall golden blades of grass burnt dark gold in the scorching sun. To his delight they were dancing and swaying in the breeze. No one was taking care of this little boy. He swirled around with wild abandonment as magic filled the air. This was the kind of magic that only little boys can only hear when they feel disconnected from love.

To discover and explore the majesty of the land was his life purpose and the secrets it contained filled his world with wonderment and joy. He loved his daily walks with Sam, his beloved dog and trusted companion. These treks were also his saving grace. The land contained majestic hay castles and playgrounds that encouraged him to explore. Without knowing how or why, he knew he was protected from the numerous dangers in nature that roamed around him. But he felt so terribly frightened and alone regarding the uncertainties of life.

Five years passed. Today was a special day. Or, it should have been. Looking into the dark pool of the mirror's reflection, he saw a stranger staring back. Luminous dark chocolate eyes peered from beneath silky black eyelashes. Black curly hair framed a beautiful face. His family members had declared, on previous occasions, that he was much too pretty to be a boy. Today was his tenth birthday. But he didn't feel much like celebrating. He wasn't sure if anyone would remember or care anyway. After a quick wash, he ventured downstairs for breakfast. There was no one to greet him, just the empty stillness that he had become accustomed to. He found no birthday present or card, nor cake with candles to commemorate his special day. He preferred to be alone anyway.

He grabbed an apple from the bowl on the table as he made his way outside and whistled for Sam. The back door closed with a loud bang behind him. He ran wildly into the forest, his mind racing. This little boy carried a secret. A terrible secret that would accompany him from childhood into adulthood. Red hot anger seethed deep inside him, chipping away at his innocence one betrayal at a time. But he was strong, he possessed the heart of a true warrior.

Nature was his true home, where he felt peace and the perfection of life. He often marvelled at the glory of nature and how it unfolded so effortlessly. Watching caterpillars morphing into butterflies and tadpoles into frogs reminded him that everything changes and evolves. The exploration of the land captured his true essence and found a home in the inner sanctum of his heart. He would spend hours scouring around native trees that held the secrets of nature's balance in the rhythm of life. Often, he would gather daisies and make daisy chains as he sat on the river bank eating his lunch. There was an innocence in his creative play, but innocence was a state of being that he could no longer feel within himself. He just felt unclean and alone.

After he trekked around the property all day, twilight silently crept in like a stranger calling. It signalled that it was time to go home. This thought filled his heart with dread. It meant looking into his mother's eyes knowing that their deep dark secret held them in bondage and fear. The bondage that it would happen again and the fear that he would have to endure it.

Mental, emotional, physical and sexual abuse was an integral part of this boy's life. It lay hidden, secretly festering behind closed doors. It was never discussed, acknowledged or healed. How can anyone heal what they don't understand? This boy was unable to ascertain which part of the torture he loathed the most. Whether it was the beatings carried out by his step-father or the betrayal of sexual abuse he endured from his mother and the innocence that was stolen. So often he lay awake at night pondering his life and why the people he trusted the most were hurting him. "Why isn't anyone looking after me? I'm a child, why do I need to endure this shocking life?" In the deep silence of a child's *pain-filled heart, no answers came to mind as he succumbed again to a restless sleep in another seemingly endless pitch-black night.*

Anger, self-loathing, fear, resentment and rage bore into John's heart. He had endured the roundabout of endless suffering during childhood and had reached adulthood by default. This was how it seemed to him. Perhaps it was sheer luck or extreme determination to beat the odds. But the abuse had left deep unhealed scars, battle wounds that wearied his soul. John didn't want to, but he knew that it was time to be honest. Earlier in the day, he had opened the locked draw and retrieved the journal he had kept secretly hidden away. Reading it didn't give him peace or solace but he knew what he needed to do. John was in love with his best friend Tala and he knew that it was time to tell her the truth.

Chapter 2

Reflections

John was a survivor of physical, emotional, mental and sexual abuse. He often repeats these words to himself but wishes they weren't true. As memories filter through his mind, honest reflections bubble to the surface. The discovery of the painful side of love has left him feeling deep anger and sadness. Inevitably, he had to live with the reality that his life hasn't turned out exactly as he had planned.

Love is eternal, so they say. The dance of love flickers and glows like a moth that is drawn to a flame. The synergy of our accumulated life experiences is born to create change within us. John lies awake thinking about where life has taken him. His fragmented life reveals itself in puzzle pieces. Once dormant, they are now scattered like silken ashes aimlessly swirling in the wind. Hidden secrets of abuse have lain dormant in his heart, stored in the intricate, hidden passage of time. Painful memories have been stuffed inside the walls of his shattered emotions.

John can honestly say that he didn't feel he was loved when he was growing up. It has been said that love's experiences ultimately present us with two possibilities. The first is the freedom to express ourselves fully. This is contained in love's nurture and care of giving and receiving. There is freedom to grow in this first discovery. Our hidden talents, gifts and abilities come to the fore to showcase who we truly are. Then we have the freedom to express ourselves fully and unconditionally to another person.

The second possibility reveals a path that hides our true self in the dark side of an unbearable reality of abuse. It is here that we became less than we should. The fear of love lures us into the sticky shadowy side of pain. A living hell ensues that inevitably reveals deep, raw emotional suffering.

The difficult life experiences and relationships we endure can be very tricky to navigate as they are fraught with dangers that lurk unseen. To understand the mysteries of the human heart is the key we need to end pain and suffering. We are then offered the opportunity to heal, to understand healthy relationships and to move on with clarity and renewed purpose.

At this stage in his life, John had to accept the choices he had made. Disempowered and disconnected to love and life is how he felt most of the time. A part of him wants to heal, yet the hidden traumatised part of him just wants to forget the hell he has lived. And so, that's exactly what he does. He buries the memories and blocks out the pain and shame. For him, it's easier that way. He tells himself it's all that he can do.

Chapter 3

Love Don't Live Here Anymore

__Tala's Diary__: The festive season celebrations were just days away and the New Year was approaching. I don't believe in making resolutions. They are just promises I will break in the end, half-truths, I tell myself. My mobile phone rang breaking the silence of my reverie. I felt slightly annoyed that someone wanted my attention but, thinking it could be important, I placed my cup of tea down on the table and answered the call.

At the sound of John's voice, I felt so joyous and happy. We talked for some time and while on the surface he seemed fine, I sensed he had something on his mind. Small talk and pleasant conversation ensued until I couldn't stand the pretence any longer.

"John, are you okay?" I asked.

"Tala, I'm fine," he replied with a tinge of sadness in his voice. He

hesitated for a moment before saying, "Tala, I would like to ask you a favour. I have written my thoughts and feelings in a journal and I would like you to read it when you have time."

I thought about it for a moment. John was asking for my help so I concluded that it must be important. I agreed to read his diary and we organised to meet the following day.

John arrived early the next morning and gave me his diary. I cleared my schedule and retreated to my meditation room so I wouldn't be disturbed. Sipping a cup of peppermint tea, I picked up John's journal and opened it. Slowly, I began to read his thoughts and feelings.

__John's Diary__: Tala is the woman who has captured my heart and soul. I feel so many conflicting emotions. There is only one way to handle the all too familiar pain of hurt and suffering I have become accustomed to so I walked across to the kitchen bench and retrieved my gardening gloves and headed out the back door. Nature, my sacred forest, was calling me.

Too many memories, too many thoughts come flooding in all at once. It was like watching wind-blown surf crashing on a wild sandy beach. Tala has captured my heart, there's no doubt in my mind, but I can't tell her how I really feel. I don't know the right words to say, to tell her that I've never felt this way about a woman before. So, I don't say anything. I don't reveal it; I can't be vulnerable. It's so easy to run and hide from my feelings. I'm not worthy of Tala. I tell myself the same fearful story every day.

As I nurture and care for the forest of native trees I have planted and cultivated with my own hands, I recalled the early days of my childhood and the horrendous pain I endured as my mother and step-father abused my innocence and trust. While I was enduring the abuse, something inside me died and my heart turned inward to find solace in a dark, unlovable place. I don't tell people about my dark secret so I pretend I'm okay, that I'm just like everyone else. It's when I'm alone that I remember. It's when I'm swamped and smothered that the negative, dark thoughts and feelings arise. And I know I'm a man, but sometimes I cry.

As I sit here writing my thoughts and feelings, I recall my life as a young man. During my early twenties, I had sex with women but connecting to my emotions and confessing abiding love wasn't on my agenda! By the time I reached my early thirties I had discovered a lot about women but not too much about myself or love. It's sad to say, but I left a few broken hearts behind.

My life progressed in a mundane way. I wasn't particularly happy or sad, I just felt numb most of the time. The week I celebrated my 35th birthday was a major turning point in my life. I hadn't fulfilled any great life purpose so on the spur of the moment I sold my possessions, withdrew all the money I had saved and bought an airline ticket to South East Asia. To some degree this trip helped to awaken something inside me but it wasn't the profound experience I had hoped for. However, I did mature. Slowly, I began to rebuild my life. I wanted to be a good, decent person. It was during this time I met my wife.

While I was travelling in Asia, my step-father died and on my return home, I was informed that I had been bequeathed a large inheritance. The money didn't fill the hole in my heart or heal the pain in my soul, but it did allow me to follow my life direction and I decided to broaden my horizons with travel.

Within a year I had booked a flight to New York, happy at the thought of creating new memorable experiences. On the third day of the trip, the tour bus arrived early to begin a day of sight-seeing in New York and I found myself seated next to an amazing woman called Anna. She was an Italian girl, a budding writer who was visiting New York for a month.

As soon as we met sparks flew, the connection was immediate. I know I fell in love with her mind. Anna was an intelligent, lovely woman. I hadn't felt this alive in a long time. During the next few weeks we spent most of our time together, getting to know each other. All too soon it was time to say goodbye. A lump formed in my throat as we hugged at the airport. We exchanged phone numbers and promised to keep in contact.

During the next twelve months, Anna and I had become great friends. The slow ember of love was simmering between us. I moved to South Australia to start a new company with the money I had inherited from my step-father and Anna and I began a long-distance relationship. We travelled back and forth between Italy and South Australia until we could arrange a visa for Anna so we could get married.

Within a few years Anna moved to Australia to live. As soon as we were married and began living together, I discovered that Anna had a quick, fiery temper. During the first year of our marriage we had blazing arguments that left me shattered and exhausted. Pride and tiredness kept me from seeing the reality of the difficult life ahead of me. I didn't want to face the truth and look at the issues we needed to address. But I think I was completely fed up and tired of living alone. Anna and I discussed divorce but decided against it. Consequently, we stayed married and endured a stormy emotional life together. It was easier that way and I wouldn't have to make an effort to heal.

Sadly, as the next few years passed, Anna stopped wanting to make love. The intimacy in our marriage ended. More anger and resentment seethed within my heart. I was only thirty-nine years old, still a young man with needs and desires and I still wanted to make love to my wife. What am I supposed to do to fulfil my sexual needs? I pondered on the dark lonely nights as I lay in our bed unable to touch the woman I loved. This was a different kind of suffering and her rejection hurt my heart even more. Small health issues appeared which I chose to ignore. Eventually, I sought medical assistance and my local GP suggested I visit a counsellor. My counsellor suggested that I learn to meditate and journal my feelings and thoughts. For a few months, I tried to meditate but found it was too difficult to quieten my mind so, instead, I found the time to journal and I planted flowers and trees in my garden. My garden grew so much that I turned the lush acreage into a forest. Spending time there, nurturing my garden kept me from going insane.

They say that everything happens for a reason. I'm not sure I believe that's true, but something wonderful happened when I least expected it. Tala walked into my office on a bright summer day. A weird feeling started hammering in my chest. It was both confronting and exciting at the same time. We spoke for a considerable length of time and discovered that we had mutual friends. Within a few weeks we were attending the same social events and getting to know each other.

Very soon a connection and attraction developed between us. We shared many common interests and life philosophies. Friendship with Tala was effortless and lots of fun. I considered my feelings about her for a long time and gave the situation a great deal of thought but eventually, I decided that I didn't want to leave my marriage and the safe way I now lived my life. I had settled and it felt comfortable. Anna was known to me, whereas, I was still getting to know Tala. Also, I wasn't prepared to leave my comfort zone.

During the next few years Tala dated other men and I sat on the sidelines feeling jealousy sear my heart whenever she was in another *man's company. I felt absolute relief when her relationships ended. I knew I was being selfish, but I didn't tell her how I felt. Love scared me, my feelings scared me. It suited me not to talk about them.*

My thoughts return to the now and a searing pain thumps at my chest. I chide myself for being selfishly indulgent. I decide that I won't allow myself to feel the depth of love I have stored in my heart for Tala. It's best that way. My wife needs me and I am content to stay where I am. Love won't hurt me anymore.

Two hours had passed since I picked up the journal. I reached for some tissues and wiped away my tears and gently placed John's diary on my lap. My mind was trying to comprehend the truth I had read. The sun was shining brightly that day but I hardly noticed. John's honesty had touched me to the core. I already knew that he loved me. I could feel it in the depth of my heart. It was also obvious in the way his eyes watched my every move and the glowing look on his face whenever I was near. Sadly, I would never be able to experience this depth of love with John.

That day I made a life-changing decision that would affect my life in a positive way. After reading John's diary, I decided it was time to leave my island paradise and relocate to Queensland. I had received a gift from reading John's journal and decided to move on with my life. The sadness I felt was intense, but the relief was immense.

As I sat in my favourite blue chair, the words I read opened a floodgate of emotions and thoughts. I cried for the love John would never know. I cried for the pain he still suffered and I cried for the loss of the love that we would never share. A deep inner knowing moved me and eventually I stopped crying. It was better to know the truth. Deep inside my heart I felt confident that I would find my Divine Union Relationship.

I knew that it was time to meet my Divine Union. John was right. I deserved more than the fear he could offer me. I could and should have it all. It was that simple. And finally, after years of feeling guilty that I was leaving him alone in his suffering, I gently closed the emotional door to John and walked into the deep sunshine, my new home in paradise in Queensland. It was calling me to my destiny and true heart's desire. My Divine Union was calling me home!

Summary: First Stage of Love – Mr Grey

Karmic Contract

Mr Grey: Yes, the emotionally unavailable Mr Grey is the first stage of love. This first stage of love is called the Karmic Contract. It can also include the Love Triangle. We have all heard the saying that two is company, three is a crowd. It certainly is. There is no room in a healthy relationship for three people to co-exist. There is no room for love to grow or to form a healthy, loving relationship and life balance. The heart cannot completely love two people at once, it's simply not possible! The list below describes the attributes of the karmic contract relationship:

- ❖ Conscious or sub-conscious fear of being alone
- ❖ Inability to change
- ❖ Financial security
- ❖ Dependence
- ❖ Commitment as co-dependence
- ❖ Heart disconnection
- ❖ Mind disconnection
- ❖ Soul disconnection
- ❖ Body identification
- ❖ Re-occurring limiting patterns and beliefs

Mr Grey will have experienced one or a combination of emotional, mental, sexual or physical traumas. He will need to keep you emotionally and or sexually present and connected to him. Control is on his mind and loving bliss is off the table.

You will find that Mr Grey hasn't healed from the first broken heart which can occur between twelve and nineteen years of age. Healing is imperative in all the stages of love, but especially in this first stage of love and it can sometimes be extensive. Encourage this man to seek professional help.

As much as you may want to support Mr Grey, ultimately, he must seek the help he needs elsewhere. YOU CANNOT SAVE HIM! Unless he can understand that he needs healing and resolution he will remain in the same conditioned pattern of pain and suffering. The first step toward healing for this man requires his self-examination.

In the first stage of love, we discover the limiting, abusive and or painful side of love – and we discover that fear conquers nothing. Only love is real. This is the seed stage, the first stage where limiting patterns and beliefs come to the fore. Fearing love is one of the most destructive things we can do. It rips at the heart and emotions, disabling people from living happy, healthy, nurtured and fulfilled loving lives. Fear creates what feels like an emotional and mental prison that endures a never-ending sentence.

Sadly, not all people leave an unhealthy or abusive relationship. It is my heart-felt wish that they could. Men and women deal with emotions differently. As men and women, we think and feel differently. Embracing this information encourages us to understand that education can be accepted and implemented.

As a young woman in my early teens, I was surrounded by very strong women. My mother, sisters, and female family members took charge. We were a female tribe. We didn't have men guiding and sharing wisdom with us. They say that men learn about relationships from the mother and women learn about relationships from the father. That's a lot of responsibility for parents. To carry this responsibility is overwhelming and more resources are needed to gain the training and support that is required. As a teenage girl,

I had no idea about how men thought, felt or behaved. They were an enigma to me.

The main focus in the first stage of love is fear. This includes fear of love, fear of being hurt, fear of rejection, and fear of enduring a broken heart. There is also fear and shame that we have hurt others in the quest for dominance and control and there is fear that we don't know who we are.

Our first relationship is with our parents. If this stage of life development holds pain, fear and suffering then education and self-healing are the first steps we need to take to embrace healing and change. Fear and love are like the two sides of a coin. If we are in a state of fear, we cannot access love. If we are in a state of love, we cannot access fear. This is simple, yet profoundly true.

It's my belief that we have to take responsibility to grow and change. It's as much our responsibility as that of our parents and care-givers. Stagnation or growth? These are the two choices we have and a choice needs to be made. Disallowing growth and change, disables people the ability to access love. Love cannot live in the dark alleyways of fear and suffering.

Love is easy! There's no doubt about it! To most of us these words can induce feelings of dread and disbelief. "What do you mean when you say that love is easy?" This is the most common question I hear when I'm teaching and explaining the concepts of the Divine Union Relationship. The most profound truth about this statement is that it's absolutely true!

Fear is hard! Fear is tricky to navigate. Abusive and dysfunctional relationships are hard. Living in a relationship that is going to end is exhausting. Living in fear, pain and suffering is soul destroying. There is no doubt about it. Some people believe that love isn't easy, so they stay in unhealthy relationships for varying reasons. The question remains: "What do we really know about love?" Some people believe that if they feel a deep connection to a partner, or a strong bond, that they have discovered love. The giddy feeling of bliss is sometimes called love. Believing that we care for someone can convince us that we have found love. These feelings are components of love, but there is so much more. I have discovered that love is profound and deeper and more intricately beautiful than I could have imagined.

The Divine Union Relationship is amazing, almost beyond belief. It's important to know that it exists, that it is real and that we can access it! The fear of love, on the other hand is soul-destroying and filled with illusion if you get trapped. It is such a complicated feeling to process. Now is the time to heal and release the bonds that restrict and keep love conditional.

The Second Stage of Love
Soul Mate – Mr McDreamy

The breathless sigh of tenderness
The look of love his eyes confess
Is she ready to find love sublime?
It's written on the heart divine
Will this man see her light?
Her sacred heart and pure delight
He has a path that he must find
It's written in the stars that shine
He teaches the wisdom of the soul
She will emerge healed and whole
So, read now this second part
Enjoy the journey as we start
To the sacred path of divine love
Illumined in the starry night above
Growth of the soul will happen for sure
Hidden within are many doors

The energy is electric when they meet
Warm is the embrace when they greet
Her soul is ready to explore
The pathway opens through golden doors
Precious soul so real, so true
Is felt and known between these two
Words of wisdom he imparts
Honourable and kind is his heart
Assisting humanity is his gift
Removing the veils of illusions shift
They walk now through the sands of time
Teacher, author and man divine
Divine man, yes, he has the key
But is he, the divine man, destined for she
The story continues in deep bliss
This second stage you won't want to miss

Chapter 4

Doctor Love

<u>Tala's Diary</u>: *Heaven on Earth, my first book had finally been published. The first copy was going to be delivered today. My cherished childhood dream had finally become a reality. Momentarily, I think about my mother, brothers and family members who have passed away. They would be so proud of my achievements. Dreams and wishes do come true. We need to believe that they can happen!*

Becoming a writer and teacher of the Divine Union Relationship was a reality. I pinched myself just to make sure I was awake and not conscious in a dream-vision experience. A small red mark appeared on my arm. Ouch! It was confirmed, I was definitely awake. It was time to stop daydreaming and get dressed. I didn't want to greet the courier in my silk pyjamas. It was such an auspicious day.

The month of June – winter time in Australia – had finally

arrived. The crisp white snow-capped mountain conveyed the image of majestic grandeur. It was glorious to look at, especially if you were viewing it from the inside of a warm, cosy kitchen. I was in no hurry to venture outside; it would be freezing. But I would go outside today as there was an important place I needed to be.

Gathering up my coat and white cashmere scarf, I walked out the door and quickly ventured to my car. It was only a ten-minute drive to the city. My daughter Bella has a special way of asking for a parking space and she will often recite, "Mother Mary full of grace, can you please find me a parking space". Today I was in a hurry so I recited the request. A gentleman indicated and reversed out of the parking space, waving goodbye. "Thank you, yes, that will do nicely," I mused to myself in love and gratitude.

As I walked up the stairs of the theatre, torrents of heavy rain began drenching the streets. I felt nervous and happy all at the same time, but I had no idea why. The theatre was a beautiful old building, architecturally designed in the late nineteenth century. My family have deep connections to this building. Some of them were dancers and actors and my mother was in charge of cleaning and repairing the costumes for the theatre company. The theatre was well-known to me and I had been part of the theatre experience since my late teens.

As I stepped inside the foyer, my friend Sharon waved to me across the room. I greeted her and within a few minutes we found our seats. It was nearly time to begin. People were speaking loudly, voices escalating in a crescendo that sounded like a swarm of buzzing bees. Wow, such excitement. I too, was feeling the same way. I managed to ignore the noise and placed my attention on the front stage. Today, the stage was set differently. There was a table, a chair and a microphone. Long draped curtains, the colour of deep-ocean blue, provided a back-drop that created calmness and serenity. Within a few minutes the lights were dimmed and a hushed silence came over the audience. The presentation was ready to begin.

Dr John Love strode across the stage purposefully, turning his head to smile at the audience. He exuded such a warm caring energy that I found myself immediately focused and ready to hear the wisdom he had to share via his lecture.

I had become aware of Dr Love's teachings when I began studying meditation and esoteric wisdom classes. I had been invited to attend the classes with a friend and discovered books, meditation and music CDs. All of my favourite things in one place. I was in heaven. The meditation teachers at the wellness centre were amazing women, dedicated in their quest to help others achieve peace and enlightenment on their path to spiritual freedom. The teachers exuded truth, honesty, compassion and genuine care for others and worked with such beauty and grace. I opened my heart to them in friendship and found a missing part of myself that I had buried for many years.

Dr Love began his lecture. He explained that in a healing workshop he attended several years ago, he had experienced a cathartic release of grief followed by an intense feeling of pure unconditional love that was overwhelming. In this experience, he discovered that love, peace and happiness were natural attributes of the soul. He was awakened.

As I listened to Dr Love's experiences, I was transfixed and amazed. There was an affiliation of experience here, different yet similar to mine. I, too, had experienced a similar awakening. As I looked at this gentleman, a knowing, a familiarity settled upon me. I can't explain it rationally, but I had a feeling I knew this man even though it was the first time I had seen him. It was an odd feeling indeed!

Two hours passed and yet it felt like only ten minutes. During the lecture, the attendees were in awe of this caring, supportive and awakened man. We were touched by his compassion and sensitive nature. Being able to touch the heart and soul of individuals in this sacred way is the sign of a truly gifted teacher and world server. We were in the presence of a divine man.

More people are coming forward to write books and teach about the soul's attributes. I smiled. I had been part of an amazing experience.

As Sharon and I walked out of the theatre, I turned to watch Dr Love talking to attendees. His face was alight with wisdom and an inner knowing that came from a deep place of knowing who he truly was. I had a feeling we would meet again. In the meantime, I would return to the wellness centre to attend meditation courses and weekend retreats.

Chapter 5

Well Made Plans

After attending Dr Love's seminar, I returned to the wellness centre to begin my training in earnest. My teacher, Margaret, invited me to join her for a cup of tea. As we sat in the kitchen, the feeling of absolute love began to fill my heart. I still couldn't explain the depth of love I felt for the teachers. I meditate daily and had been doing so for many years but meeting these evolved soul teachers gave me a deepening sense of peace, happiness and joy that I hadn't experienced in a very long time. There was an inner contentment in my heart, a sense that I had finally come home.

While drinking peppermint tea together, Margaret talked to me about the significance of their soul teachings. They were so familiar to my soul and my own inner knowing and I resonated deeply with the teachings. I had been living soul conscious for many years. Margaret continued to question me about my own wisdom training and we chatted for two hours. Or, I thought we were simply chatting. At the end of our wonderful conversation, Margaret exclaimed, "Congratulations, you have just completed the Foundation Course." The course usually takes seven weeks to complete and she had simply filled in the relevant knowledge that I was missing. Wow, I wasn't expecting that!

Over time, I participated in a few other study courses and then seriously considered becoming a soul teacher. I believed that Margaret thought it could be a calling, a deeper connection to my life purpose. After class one evening, we talked openly and honestly about the requirements of becoming a teacher. The head teaching positions were held by women. Men could share wisdom and hold classes and workshops, but women were the primary teachers.

My heart, body, soul and mind were being pulled in two different directions. On one hand, the thought of becoming a soul teacher was humbling and filled my heart and soul with joy. Simultaneously, I had pledged to become a teacher of the Divine Union Relationship. I pondered and considered my options. Finally, I made the decision.

It was with a heavy heart I explained to Margaret that my life purpose of being a Divine Union Relationship teacher was in direct conflict with becoming a spiritual teacher at the wellness centre. I had to follow my heart and the promise I had made. Healing the family, assisting women to find the courage to leave unhealthy or destructive relationships and assisting them to access the Divine Union Relationship was the driving force of my life purpose and it was deeply important for me to pursue my current life path. Within a week, with a heavy heart I quietly shut the door on the wellness centre.

Chapter 6

Loving Friends

For the next seven years, I conducted research and worked with people to assist them to release limiting patterns and outdated beliefs. I also relayed the teachings of the Divine Union Relationship. I knew that I had made the right choice, but I continued to care deeply for the meditation teachers, they felt like my soul-sisters. Whenever I attended expos or health and wellness events I would see them setting up their booths. They would walk around quietly, with deep love shining from their eyes and would offer everyone they met a radiant smile. Whenever we met, we would smile at each other and their eyes conveyed that they were at peace and supported my decision. And yet, I felt a sense of incompleteness knowing that I couldn't merge the two.

As destiny decreed, a lady called Gwyneth would encourage me to re-think my decision. She was a distant friend and we would see each other at social events and often enjoy lively conversation. A woman in her late sixties, she exuded confidence, vitality, wisdom and a dynamic cheeky sense of humour.

One particular Saturday afternoon we met at friend's birthday party. Gwyneth told me that she had found the wellness centre and invited me to attend a meditation class with her. "I have a feeling you will love it!" she exclaimed. Little did she know how accurate she was. I politely declined and moved on to talk to other friends.

A year later we met at another social event. Gwyneth had been attending advanced classes and was preparing to travel to India for more training. When she pleaded with me to attend a meditation class with her, I explained to her that I had left and my reasons for doing so. "You don't have to become a teacher," she implored. "Just come along and keep me company." I told her I would think about it.

I seriously considered returning to a meditation class as I missed the friendships I had formed with the teachers and students. A profound sense of love and peace always permeated my heart when I was with them and my life always seemed to flow in a more balanced and peaceful way. So, I called Gwyneth and told her I would attend meditation class with her, but that was all I could offer. She accepted my decision with glee. "We are going to have so much fun," she exclaimed. She arranged to collect me at 7.00 pm the following evening.

When I ventured into the meditation class, the same feeling of peace, love and joy encircled my heart. I quickly took my seat and looked across the room to see one of the teachers beaming a huge smile at me. Other students nodded in friendliness and offered welcoming smiles. I looked at the photo of the esteemed spiritual leader hanging on the wall and those magical eyes seemed to be smiling at me as if to say, "I knew you would return one day. Welcome home!"

Meditation class had been moved and was now being conducted in the home of Ally, an incredible woman who mothered everyone and, as I would soon discover, was also an incredible cook. Before I knew it, I was being invited to afternoon tea with Ally and Gwyneth.

Enjoying tea and sweets then escalated to being invited to share breakfast and I started to again revel in the teachings I had loved so much. Gwyneth and I had developed an incredible bond of friendship that I treasured and Ally created a mothering bond with me that I desperately needed. We spent hours talking and meditating. I remember sitting around the kitchen table one morning enjoying a bowl of delicious pumpkin soup for breakfast and one of the teachers shared a story and we all laughed together in complete unison. Never had I felt the bond of sisterhood as deeply as I did that day. It was idyllic and blessed to say the least.

Six months later, I entered the meditation class to find a group of people talking excitedly and a young lady asked me if I had heard of Dr John Love. Hmm! I certainly had. She informed me that he was conducting a three-day retreat on a beautiful island. "You need to speak to Ally," she said. "There are only a few tickets available."

Here we go again, I thought to myself. It was decision time. Attending the retreat and hearing the wisdom and teaching of Dr Love was only going to foster my love of soul teaching at a deeper level. Did I really want to put myself in that position again? I decided that I didn't and although it took a great deal of self-control, I didn't buy a ticket to attend the retreat.

For weeks, those planning to attend were talking excitedly about the upcoming retreat and meeting Dr Love. I understood their enthusiasm and encouraged them to take notes and absorb the wisdom he had to impart. I often commented that the retreat would assist their growth and awareness in ways they would understand later.

The week of the retreat finally arrived. Due to preparations for a family gathering, I had missed two meditation classes, but I had also needed some time away from all the excitement and talk about the retreat. Inwardly, I was disappointed that I would not be attending. Gwyneth and I arranged to meet for morning tea early in the week and after consuming a cup of peppermint tea and a delicious piece of chocolate slice, the topic of conversation turned to the weekend retreat with Dr Love.

"You should be attending the retreat you know," chided Gwyneth. For the past two weeks, the same thought had repeatedly occurred to me but I didn't tell anyone how I felt.

"I'd really like to attend but there aren't any tickets available," I replied.

"Well, if it's meant to be then a ticket will become available," said Gwyneth. She was right, so I decided to call Ally and ask if she had any tickets available.

But before I had a chance to call her, my mobile phone rang. "Hello," I said.

"It's Ally here. I've just received a call from a lady who has cancelled her reservation to attend the three-day retreat with Dr Love. I thought of you immediately and wondered if you would like to go?" The woman who had originally purchased the ticket said that she felt that someone else was meant to go in her place and that person would be offered the ticket.

I thought for a moment and replied, "I was just about to call you and ask if you had a ticket available. But I didn't think for one minute that you would have one."

"You are the one who is meant to be there," said Ally.

I quickly agreed and paid Ally for the ticket. Now it was time to pack. I was meant to attend this retreat and the experiences I would have would be breathtaking.

Chapter 7

Facets of Love

Gwyneth arrived at 4.00 pm on Friday afternoon to take me to the retreat. We waved goodbye to my children and set off happy and relaxed, looking forward to the adventure of a life-time. Gwyneth knew I had attended a lecture given by Dr Love many years ago and that the experience had a significant impact on me. A man of wisdom, intelligence and community respect had confirmed the same principles, knowledge and soul wisdom I understood.

We arrived at the retreat centre before dinner time as attendees were arriving from four Australian states. Gwyneth was staying with the soul teachers while I was to share a room with another attendee. I ventured into the main meeting room and greeted other guests. With joy, I recognised some of the other students.

Once we had settled in, Gwyneth and I went for a long walk

along the beach. We walked past Dr Love and a large group of women who had gathered around him, talking and laughing together. As we passed the group, Dr Love looked at me and a slight glimmer of recognition swept across his face. He smiled and I felt myself blush.

"Why are you flustered?" asked Gwyneth.

"I have no idea," I replied. We continued our walk along the beach in silence. I had no intention of discussing something I didn't understand myself. All too soon it was time to return for dinner.

The smell of vegetarian food filled the room with an amazing aroma. The food was absolutely delicious and plentiful. Dessert was a selection of Ally's favourite delicious sweet treats, a feast for the eyes and comfort for the soul. Once dinner was finished, we were asked to meet in the main meeting area.

Placed around the room was a selection of large plush comfortable couches, chairs and recliners that allowed everyone a perfect front-view of Dr Love so that he could teach and walk around freely. I chose a large recliner near the front of the room. Usually, I like to hide in the background but I was feeling brave and decided to do something different that would take me out of my comfort zone.

Dr Love was ready to start the introduction to the retreat. He explained the course content to be discussed during the next three days. It was extensive and for the first time I truly understood that I really was meant to attend. At this stage I couldn't imagine being anywhere else.

It was 8.00 pm on Friday evening when we began to meditate.

Dr Love played a CD track from Bliss called A Hundred Thousand Angels, one of my favourite songs. I found myself floating outside myself instead of feeling the state of oneness and deep connection that I usually experience in meditation. I was startled when I heard the sound of his voice reminding us that it was time to return to the room.

Dr Love asked if anyone would like to share their meditation experience. As I listened to the responses, I could already feel the attendees beginning to form a bond of trust and openness with him. I smiled. Yes, I knew that feeling very well.

I was sitting quietly listening to what other people had to say when I sensed two eyes boring into the side of my face. Blushing, I looked up to see Dr Love staring at me. He looked at me with soulful eyes and said, "Tala, would you like to share your experience with us?" My first thought was no, absolutely not. Then I remembered that I had decided to attend this retreat to have new experiences.

Slowly, I began to share the details of my meditation experience. A quiet hush moved across the room and the attendees waited patiently for me to continue talking. I explained that I had found myself out of my body and quickly realised I had travelled to a higher dimension. At least, that's how it seemed to my mind's limited perspective. I could sense the presence of angels. The degree of angelic love is very difficult to describe and our human language doesn't have the means to do it justice. I understood that angelic love is the language of light, colour and sound vibration. I took a deep breath and sat still for a moment. The silence seemed to stretch into eternity, but in reality, only a few moments had passed. Without warning, I felt an angel move and stand by my side, enveloping my auric field with light. It was gold light, sprinkled with white light particles so infinitely small that they resembled the brilliance of a sparkling prism of the purest diamond cluster. The light blinded my eyes for a moment and then I reminded myself to breathe, to take a big deep breath and to let the love I was feeling flow within and through my body. I was then encouraged to open my heart centre and to allow the love and light of the angel to flow out and into the room.

At that exact moment, my body began to vibrate and I saw a violet and gold light had covered the room like a soft cashmere blanket of love. The feelings flooding through me felt soft and pure, almost effortless in this higher state of consciousness. I knew that I had been in this vision state for quite a long time and then I heard Dr Love say that it was time to open our eyes. I had not been expecting that at all.

People were smiling at me and then they all started talking at once. Most people believed in the concept of angels and were delighted to hear of my experience. Others were sceptical and some were non-committal. The attendees who believed in angels were convinced that they are a real presence in our physical world, here to bring comfort, support and love in our everyday lives.

Dr Love looked at me for a few more minutes and then thanked me for sharing my experience with the group and for the flurry of conversation that occurred. The evening ended on a high note and everyone went to bed feeling that magical experiences were going to be plentiful during the next few days.

As I prepared for bed, I looked in the mirror as I removed my make-up. I hadn't ventured out in public without it for twenty years. The make-up wipe swished across my face, removing foundation, eye-shadow, mascara and lipstick. I hesitated as I brushed the soft white cloth over the left-side of my face. The scars I sustained during my birth left me feeling naked, exposed, vulnerable and ugly. None of these feelings filled me with confidence or surety. Yet, within my heart today I felt the stirring of a new, different feeling. Something I couldn't explain had happened in the last few hours. Happiness and joy exuded from me. Little did I know that I would discover more about myself during the next three days than I believed was possible.

As I climbed into bed I slipped my ear plugs in my ears and played 'A Hundred Thousand Angels' on my portable CD player. The melody was beautiful and soothing. Suddenly, a deafening sound pounded on the roof, reminding me of a herd of elephants thundering across the plains in Africa in a David Attenborough television documentary. A few minutes later an attendee stood in the doorway and explained it was just the local possums playing their nightly game of "let's see how many humans we can frighten". Good job guys, I thought to myself. It was time for sleep, and I was definitely going to need to be focused and clear-minded tomorrow.

When morning arrived, the sun's rays peeked through the sheer curtains. I quickly showered and dressed, predominantly in white. Since I was a child I had always felt light and fresh when I dressed in white clothes. As I applied my make-up, I decided to put on a light foundation and a little eyeshadow but no eye-liner or lipstick. I still needed foundation to cover my scars and it was unthinkable for me not to wear it. I studied my reflection and was happy with my decision and headed to the main meeting room to enjoy breakfast.

Large tables were laden with delicious food from traditional home-made pumpkin soup simmering in a pot, porridge and freshly cooked toast to delicious summer berries. "Ah, what shall we eat?" asked each attendee. This was a discussion we would entertain each morning.

I selected porridge and fruit and headed to a table where some attendees were already eating and chatting easily. They waved and encouraged me to join them. As I ate my breakfast, I breathed in the fresh country air, soaking up the energy of nature until we were asked to make our way to the meeting room to begin the first day.

Chapter 8

First Facet

Meditation began promptly at 10.00 am. We chose a couch or chair and settled into a comfortable position. Dr Love arrived dressed in white clothes and looking refreshed and ready to begin the morning session. "Please call me John," Dr Love suggested as we settled down to begin the morning session. As we listened to another amazing selection of music, I found myself floating in what can only be described as a realm or world of love and light. This was really odd as I only do this in dream-visions when I'm asleep. Within a few minutes I heard Dr John tell us that it was time to return. Or so I thought. In reality, we had been meditating for half an hour.

Where did the time go? Or more importantly where did I go? I wondered. Odd things were happening to me that I didn't understand. Thankfully, other attendees were only too happy to share their experiences so I remained silent and the morning session passed quickly. All too soon lunch was ready to be served!

Numerous varieties of vegetarian food were set out on long trestle tables. My digestive system is sensitive to dairy and gluten and to my surprise I found that I tolerated vegetarian food exceptionally well. We consumed a beautiful lunch and, of course, the sweet treats we indulged in were divine. Within an hour we finished eating our lunch and returned for the afternoon session. New experiences were about to begin.

Meditation students who attended the wellness centre were taught to look at each other in a specific way. You gaze at another person and connect to them by looking deeply into their eyes, bypassing the body and personality and looking directly into the soul. When you experience this for this first time it can be quite confronting and uncomfortable. But it was easy for me. I had always been able to see the soul, to connect with another person's real essence, ever since I was a child.

We were divided into groups of six and the soul gazing began. Within a few minutes, some group members were laughing and giggling, unable to sustain the gaze, using laughter as a method to avoid being seen and feeling vulnerable. It was easier to giggle than allow another person to gaze inside, to see who you really are. Sensing discomfort, the teachers gathered within each group and helped to settle them. Being able to accomplish soul connection was part of the soul teaching.

Then the most amazing thing occurred. When group members removed the feeling of discomfort and vulnerability they were able to complete the exercise. Some people discussed what they were feeling and seeing. Most indicated that they felt warmth and love in their hearts. Some said that they could feel or sense colour and some indicated a profound sense of peace and unconditional love.

In the next stage of experiential teaching, we were asked to stand facing each other in two straight lines and were instructed to look at the person opposite us and gaze into their soul. Because I was an accomplished meditator and had been a previous student, I was able to do this without effort. The next step consisted of moving from side to side like a dance. Looking into the soul is akin to dancing. Soul dancing is subtle, gentle, open hearted and requires a great degree of trust. As we moved in perfect formation, I allowed my soul to connect with as many people as I could and found that it helped the other students enormously. It's unbelievable to see another person's real essence, to see without prejudice what they really look like, to see true beauty. This is an amazing skill and a true gift to share with others.

Dr John joined the group and moved with effortless grace. As an enlightened soul, his contribution was greatly appreciated. I felt his presence near me and then it was my turn to face him. Initially, I was a little dazed. I was comfortable and open with women gazing into my soul but I was taking tentative steps in allowing a man to do this. My heart had healed with the loss of my Divine Union essence Andre, but I was still taking tentative steps forward in the realm of the heart. Unbeknown to me, I was learning new information concerning the aspects of the Divine Union Relationship.

Dr John was described by other women as very handsome. While I agreed with them on a physical level, I sensed there was something more, something deeper I was meant to learn. At this stage I had no idea what that might be, but still, I felt there was something deeper I was being taught.

Once I let down my guard, Dr John opened fully and let me see the essence of his soul. The sight was breathtaking. Unconditional love oozed out of his eyes in streams of love and light. I definitely didn't want to take my eyes off him and I didn't want him to leave! But not in the way that sounds or you might think. He was elevating me to higher parts of myself and to a new teaching. He was teaching me to connect more deeply with my soul. There was a subliminal connection here, nothing to do with being a man and a woman and something inside me had opened up, something more expansive than I had ever known before. All too soon, it was time for the afternoon session to end. Dr John smiled at me as he passed by and returned to the front of the room.

The early evening meditation was set to begin before dinner. As we settled into our chairs I remember thinking that I felt unencumbered and free. The familiar feeling began and I lost all sense of time, and spaciousness was everywhere. Dr John's voice, soothing and quiet, was reminding me that we are infinite souls of peace and love. Yes, once again, it was time to return. Dr John bought the session to a close, bid us farewell and said that he looked forward to another wonderful day tomorrow. We too, felt the same way and nodded in agreement.

After dinner, we gathered in groups and discussed the events we had experienced during the day. A few of the attendees commented on my ease with meditation and group exercises. I quietly explained that I had briefly studied the teachings. "Ah, that explains it," they replied and I was content to leave it at that.

Gwyneth and I sat together during dinner and as twilight approached we took a walk along the beach. The sound of birds chirping and the lapping of waves on the ocean shore made my heart sing. A glorious sunset draped the sky with colours of crimson and gold. We marvelled at nature's originality and effortless display of perfection and as we walked our conversation returned to the events of the day.

"How are you feeling now?" asked Gwyneth.

I took a few deep breaths and gathered my thoughts before I answered her question. I wasn't sure how I felt or what had happened but I trusted Gwyneth so I talked to her about my experiences. "A myriad of feelings really, soul gazing was amazing today and I enjoyed contributing to the group experience."

It was beginning to get dark and Gwyneth suggested we should return to the cabin. As we walked back along the beach, the full moon was bright, reflecting light and radiating its own magic across the moonlit sea.

Chapter 9

Second Facet

The next morning dawned bright and sunny as we prepared to begin a new day. I sprang out of bed, showered and dressed in my white shirt and trousers. Some of the group members attended a teaching class followed by a 6.00 am meditation class conducted by the teachers. Others went down to the beach and joined a tai chi class. I preferred to go outside and headed toward a beautiful willow tree in the garden. My morning journaling was and still is a daily practice and my morning ritual. It is a perfect way for me to start the day.

At 8.00 am, group members gathered for breakfast. People were talking amongst themselves and, of course, the ladies wanted to talk about Dr John. I am not one to sit around and partake in general gossip so I began to strategize an escape plan. As if she could read my thoughts, Gwyneth approached the table and asked me if I would like to accompany her on a quick walk along the beach. I nodded in agreement and we left the group. We walked in silence for half an hour, each of us lost in our own thoughts. It was the therapeutic aid we needed before we began the morning session.

At 10.00 am, we ventured inside to find our seats and Dr John arrived ready to commence a new day of teaching. We started with a meditation and once more the sound of beautiful music created from the heavenly spheres reached our ears. We were led by Dr John into a guided meditation, a garden in nature. The scene was straight out of a Monet landscape painting. Stunning imagery and iridescent pastel colours danced and played around my mind and the experience was blissful. More teaching of soul awareness occurred and then it was time for lunch.

After the lunch break, we sat in groups of four and talked about soul growth and utilised our personal experiences as experiential learning tools. This was the first time I had shared with another person, outside my family, that I had experienced and survived a serious domestic violence situation. I shared how I had healed, resolved and moved on from my ex-husband. Sadly, the experience revealed that I was being seen as different from the others somehow. Being labelled different was the exact opposite of what I wanted to share. It was important to me that other people understand that we all possess incredible inner strength, resolve and wisdom. It's about learning how to tap into that. I'm not a special person in any way. I feel deep love in my heart for my children, family and humanity. Simple!

A wonderful couple, my friends Mark and Sienna had also attended the course. During the afternoon session, they shared with the group that they had brought their drums with them and it was decided we would have a drumming session later that evening. Music? My favourite pastime. I didn't need any encouragement. The idea of playing drums and singing was joy to my heart and soul. Dr John recounted more of his life and teachings and the afternoon passed quickly and the second day session came to a close.

We enjoyed a wonderful dinner and finally, it was time to play the drums. Dr John had retired to rest and relax after the day's teachings. Tomorrow was the last day of the retreat. The sound of twenty deep-base, resonating drums pounding together is spine-tingling. I allowed other group members to experience this bliss first. Then it was my turn. A gentle beat began as the group sat in a perfect circle. Mark, an experienced musician and drum-maker, led us in a song of creativity, complexity and rhythm. We loved it. As the song evolved and we became more involved, the rhythm beat expanded and the volume with it.

My inner goddess moved to the fore and I found myself enjoying and participating wholeheartedly in this event in a way that I don't usually. What was happening to me? I was shedding old layers of outdated patterns and beliefs where I was frightened to let people see the real me. The teaching I had received from Dr John was starting to have a dramatic positive effect.

I was having an amazing time, sharing music and soul connection with this group of soul conscious people. I loved having soul experiences. Suddenly, a warm heat started to move from my heart and it encircled me completely. I threw my head back and laughed with a genuine child-like happiness. Without warning, or knowing why, I turned to my left to see Dr John beaming at me. Unbeknown to me he had returned when he heard the music and wanted to participate. Instead of feeling small, insecure and alone I allowed him to see the real me and I returned his smile wholeheartedly. It was an experience of the soul and the joy of participating in life's simple pleasure of music.

Within a few hours, we had finished drumming our collective song and the drums were returned to their cases. Someone joked that we should release the song on the radio. We all laughed. When Fiona, one of the young women attending, mentioned she had brought her guitar, some group members pleaded with her to play a song. A favourite tune that most of us knew was decided upon and Ally wrote the lyrics on three large sheets of butcher paper for those who didn't. Then she asked for volunteers from the audience.

The old familiar pattern of thinking "please don't pick me" resurfaced and I tried to hide at the back of the room.

All too soon I heard Dr John say, "Ally, I will hold the lyrics; I will take one sheet."

Ally looked around the room and spotted me hiding in the background. "Tala, yes, I'm sure you would love to volunteer."

My face blushed crimson-red as I reluctantly made my way to the front of the room. Dr John was grinning broadly at me as if to say, "Well, if you are going to shine like a bright star and then try to hide your real self, it doesn't work that way." Ally volunteered to hold the last sheet and so the music began.

I took the sheet of paper from Ally, giving her a wry smile, and refused to look at Dr John who was still grinning, enjoying the moment immensely. Ally moved slightly and I found myself standing beside the very debonair Dr John. Fiona began to pluck the guitar strings and produced a beautiful, soulful melody. A haunting sweet tune reverberated effortlessly around the room as we fell into a hushed reverie. Her beautiful voice echoed in our ears and we were transfixed. The lyrics contained a special message for me. The words indicated that shining our light, our true essence is vital to self-healing, self-acceptance and self-love. Yes, this really was my song.

For a moment, I forgot where I was and enjoyed the experience, concentrating on the fact that I was being helpful. Standing at the front of the room was fine and the butterflies swirling in my stomach had stopped. I found, to my amusement, that I was having a great time, just being myself. Dr John was teaching me that I was absolutely fine and that it was perfectly acceptable to give myself permission to shine.

When the song finished and the applause quietened down, Fiona did something out of character. "Okay," she said, "this time, let's all sing together."

Now, singing in public is not what I do at all! I had a fear of being ridiculed and rejected so I definitely wasn't going to subject myself to that. Fiona turned to me and smiled a smile so heart-warming that I thought my heart would melt and she whispered, "It's okay, just open your mouth and sing the words, the rest will be fine." Fiona took a deep breath and began to sing. Soon after, Dr John began to sing as well. Ally joined in with gusto and I stood there stunned at all that was unfolding around me.

I opened my mouth and words emerged. Dr John and Ally grinned as I softly began to sing the words I knew so well. By the second verse I was singing louder. Fiona looked behind and gave me the biggest smile of encouragement, nodding her head for me to continue. By the chorus I had fully joined in and was enjoying myself immensely. As we finished, everyone was cheering and clapping.

Fiona whispered, "Tala, you have a really lovely voice, you need to sing more."

The elation I felt was boundless. I was deliriously happy having conquered one of my greatest fears as I shifted a limiting pattern and belief about myself.

The night finally came to an end and as we said goodnight, Gwyneth commented that the teaching and meditation classes would begin at 4.00 am the next morning. She invited me to attend and as I prepared for bed I gave some thought to her offer. I couldn't re-develop a close bond with the spiritual teachings as I had another life purpose to fulfil. No immediate answer came to mind so I went to bed with unresolved feelings. In my muddled state, I forgot to set the alarm. Unbeknown to me, a greater plan was quietly emerging.

Chapter 10

Third Facet

The last day of the retreat had arrived. Something touched my arm and I jumped up quickly, hoping that it wasn't a large spider keeping me company in my bed! I was relieved to see the shadow of a woman standing beside me encouraging me to get dressed. It was 3.50 am and the group meditation class was ready to begin. In a split-second decision, I decided to go, that I was meant to be there. I quickly scrambled out of bed.

I only had time for a very quick wash to freshen my body and as I dressed, I realised to my dismay that I didn't have time to apply my make-up. For a moment, I thought about climbing back into the warmth and comfort of my bed. More inner shifts were taking place and I chided myself for being scared to feel vulnerable and real. I headed out, hoping the lights in the meditation room would be dim so that no one would look at me too closely.

Dressed in a white tee-shirt, black track-pants and white joggers and carrying a light jumper over my shoulders, I crept silently into the meditation room. As I entered, the light nearly blinded me. Great, I thought, so much for hiding in a dark room. I closed my eyes and sat quietly. The 4.00 am hour of nectar had arrived.

The meditation teachers, dignified and serene were sitting in deep meditation with their eyes open, gazing softly. The door opened and Dr John's tall manly essence filled the room. Soul connection began and I felt the love, care, respect and genuine compassion radiate through the eyes of these special women. Dr John sat in quiet respect and connected with each one of us in turn. I remember experiencing the effects of the unconditional love he was radiating so startling and pure that I nearly fell off my chair. I also forgot that I wasn't wearing any makeup. A unique feeling of deliciousness came over me, the understanding from a deep human level that I was being seen for who I really was. The meditation class was finally concluded and it was time to leave.

As we stopped outside the meditation room to put on our shoes a few members gathered to talk to Dr John. He always radiated humour, warmth and unconditional love to everyone. My shoelace had loosened so I lingered to fasten it. Gwyneth and I found ourselves at the back of the group. Momentarily, Dr John stopped to talk to one of the teachers and left the group. Within a few minutes he was striding beside us, smiling and asking how we were enjoying the retreat. It was the first time we had spoken.

His voice sounded like the tinkling of bells and it spoke directly to my heart. It was a pleasure to talk to him. Then he did something that left me completely dumbstruck. As we approached the door to the kitchen he stopped and stood just a few inches from me. Then he smiled a dazzling smile and gazed at me. I wasn't wearing any makeup. My face was bare, foundation free, my scars were visible to the world. My eyes were uncovered. I was real and exposed, just as mother nature intended. He studied my face and he gazed at me. He searched my face for what seemed like an eternity.

And then I realised what was happening. He was connecting to the real inner me. He could see who I really was. Then he smiled deeper, a glorious smile that sent shivers up and down my spine. In that moment, I felt divine love pouring into me in waves of unconditional love and bliss. Heat in my heart chakra burst through my chest and a fire flamed to access new energy. I felt so beautiful and alive in a way that no human perfection could ever understand or accept. Oh, what a feeling, a miracle of real beauty and truth!

Eventually, other people began looking at us and some women were sending uncomplimentary looks my way. I felt uncomfortable and wanted to end the conversation, whereas, Dr John was casually leaning on the pole and showing no signs of wanting to move in a hurry. I mumbled an excuse and finally went inside to have breakfast. The conversation had ended but the shifts within my soul kept happening.

The last morning session of our retreat had arrived. We gathered for our usual morning meditation class and when I looked to the front of the room Dr John smiled at me. My heart melted, for just a moment. We gathered in pairs during the morning session. There was more information to be given regarding the teachings of the soul. A woman standing beside me asked if we could work together and I happily agreed. As we began our session together I noticed her gazing at Dr John with a look of admiration and something else I couldn't quite define. We talked and completed the exercises as instructed and then she leaned across my shoulder and in a quiet, secretive voice said, "Dr John can put his shoes under my bed any day. Making love with him would be out of this world."

My initial reaction was one of shock and then I began to laugh. "Wow," I thought. And then it dawned on me that she was being very present and human and sharing an honest, real sexual yearning. I smiled and conceded that, yes, I could see that he was a very attractive man. All too soon the morning session ended and it was time for lunch.

Our final afternoon session was ready to commence and I was feeling a mixture of elation and sadness that our time together was coming to an end. Dr John was ready to conduct our final meditation. It was a beautiful way to complete our time together as a group. We had been nourished heart, body, soul and mind. We had made new friends, reacquainted with old friends and learnt much about our soul, our inner essence and our being. Before commencing the meditation, Dr John asked each one of us to share any experiences or positive feelings we had discovered during the retreat.

For the next hour, everyone shared their experiences and what the retreat had meant to them on a personal level. Some people shared feelings of connection, bliss, peace and love. Others shared altered experiences and the feeling of belonging and connecting as they experienced life at the soul level. Everyone agreed that they had received new tools they would include in their everyday lives. In unison, we all thanked Dr John and the spiritual teachers who had touched our lives in such a loving and positive way. We were all filled with so much gratitude and love for them.

With gentle honour and deep connection in his heart Dr John said it was time to begin our final meditation. We gathered in a very large circle. The sound of angelic voices crooning through time and space created sacred energy that filled the air. I was meditating deeply. Unconditional love bathed me softly and I sensed the familiar experience of being free and boundless in a sea of loving peace and joy. Finally, Dr John spoke gently, bringing us back to conclude the retreat. We had shared a sacred space and it took some time for everyone to re-orient their senses. One last time, I looked at Dr John, sitting directly opposite me and at the same, exact moment, he looked across at me.

Worlds seem to collide, time and space ceased to exist as we connected on a deep-soul subliminal level. I was sitting comfortably on the chair but I couldn't seem to move and I really didn't want to. Everyone was sitting quietly, waiting for Dr John to speak. But he didn't. The long seconds turned into a minute. My soul could feel and sense our past history. We were soul-mates. A sense of joy and wonderment encased us in a state of innocence and simplistic, pure rapture.

As the minute turned into two, people were looking at each other slightly confused, not knowing what was happening. Then, simultaneously, everyone looked at Dr John before turning their heads as one to look at me. Physicality ceased to exist, we were two souls connecting as one, just like the fathomless depths of the ocean, we were seeing the perfection of our soul presence. I was aware that it was an honour of the highest degree and I was truly humbled to have experienced it.

Sensing the degree of panic and confusion on the group's faces, I moved my gaze away from Dr John. They seemed relieved and quickly went over to him to say farewell and offer further thanks.

He smiled, a smile so incredibly sweet. He wasn't my Divine Union but an integral part, a beautiful teacher who had helped and encouraged me to strip away my fears and illusions of self-doubt. I had found another piece to the puzzle and I was content to float on a cloud of bliss for a very long time.

Now I possessed the information and wisdom I needed to know to take me to the next stage of love.

Summary: Second Stage of Love – Mr McDreamy

Soul Mate

Mr McDreamy is the second stage of love and the soul-mate relationship. Dr John is certainly a very dreamy man in every way. A soul-mate relationship is such a beautiful and extraordinary relationship. But what is a soul-mate relationship? A soul-mate can be found in a romantic or platonic relationship between couples. It can be a familial relationship between mother and daughter or father and son or vice versa. It can be accessed in a loving connection between friends. The soul-mate stage of romantic love is extraordinarily beautiful and fulfilling. This loving relationship can endure for a lifetime and can shift easily into the Divine Union Relationship.

How do you know if you are experiencing a soul-mate romantic relationship?

- ❖ The connection is so strong that you are drawn to them in a way you have never experienced before
- ❖ You understand each other better than anyone else
- ❖ You love each other unconditionally
- ❖ You experience an intense connection and emotional feelings
- ❖ You offer each other security and protection
- ❖ You cannot walk away from each other easily
- ❖ You look into each other's eyes with a high level of comfort and confidence
- ❖ You share non-verbal communication
- ❖ You share a special loving bond
- ❖ You affirm the best in each other

❖ Peace, calmness and happiness abound when you are with each other

❖ You assist each other to become your authentic self

❖ You become so much more aware of the beauty in life because you have been given a great gift of connection and will always be thankful

Dr John gave me an amazing, precious and rare gift. I was shown my soul, my real essence and I became aware of and more deeply connected to the beauty in life. I knew who I was and I opened my heart to my true essence, my authentic self. As I learnt how to face my phobias and fears head on, I was encouraged to acknowledge my authentic self.

The simple teaching of the second stage of love stipulates that if you are involved in a soul-mate romantic relationship, then revel in it and discover more fully the joy and wonderment contained in this love.

If your soul-mate relationship ends, then this will be devastating to endure. The pain will be felt deeply. Therefore, if this occurs, it is imperative to heal through this stage of transition. The next stage reveals the evolution to the Divine Union Relationship. Remember, we always have the final say. The choice is given freely and is ours alone to make.

The Third Stage of Love
Heart Soul – Mr Unavailable

Guitar melodies fill the air
To herald this love beyond compare
Lyrics penned upon the heart
A connection deep, a beautiful spark
A treasure of the real, pure kind
Thoughts of love are on his mind
Through the sands of time he will explore
The path of love he searches for
Destiny whispers in the air
The path endures, the reality flares
And all the while now love roams
As she sips her hot chocolate foam
Two eyes lock across a crowded room
At the first sight of him she swoons
But is this feeling a soul-mate domain
Or is he her Divine Union to claim?

The next stage of love is ready to start
An unknown place to impart
In the depths of love and light
The deepest touch and sparks ignite
And roar into a mighty flame
Her heart is set to love again
She will look at him with awe
But is he the one her heart divine searches for?
Is he the one who claims her heart?
Is he the one who can impart?
The teachings of this love divine
Two hearts and souls need to combine
Tall, dark and oh, so handsome is he
This beautiful man of divinity
Keep reading now we do implore
He rocks her world to the core
You really won't be able to resist
Do they seal their connection with a kiss?
Kiss and tell, oh no, not me
Keep reading now, just wait and see

Chapter 11

My Lucky Stars

Researching is my passion. However, it involves copious amounts of reading. I loved learning the intricate concepts about the Divine Union Relationship. It was like collating puzzle pieces and learning how to combine them in an intricate pattern. I even wished upon a star for assistance with my life path. Although I was unsure what steps to take, my inner knowing seemed to be pulling me in a particular direction.

Closing the door to the wellness centre community was heart-wrenching as I felt a strong desire to see my friends. "Chin up," I could hear my mother say. She was a firm believer in getting on with life and not feeling sorry for oneself. I knew if I could cultivate one of her pearls of wisdom, everything would turn out just fine.

The third stage of love was ready to begin. Dr John had

provided me with first-hand experience of the platonic soul-mate experience. And as I closed the door on the past and left it securely bolted behind me, I felt confident. New experiences were soon to unfold.

It was time to broaden my horizons and take the next steps of my life purpose path. As I was busy conducting my own research, I wasn't looking for a career, just a part-time position two days a week and I secured a role as an administration officer in the non-profit sector at our local hospital. The job description stated that the company raised funds for medical research. Being of service was on my agenda so this role suited me perfectly.

Our destiny path has a funny way of showing up when we least expect it. The path that led me to finding this role was meant to be. Despite having attended my scheduled monthly appointment only the week before, I received a letter from the job seeker network in which I was enrolled. I remember at the time thinking it was odd but I was keen to secure a job so I attended the scheduled appointment.

When I entered the reception area for the second week in a row, I was greeted by someone I did not know. The lady introduced herself as Sue, shook my hand and asked me to accompany her into her office. Her smile was warm and assuring, immediately putting me at ease. She asked me to take a seat and as I did so she looked at her computer and read the notes on my file. Within a few minutes she looked up with a puzzled expression on her face and said, "I have no idea why you are here. The computer has generated a meeting appointment for you but you have already complied for this month by attending your meeting last week. There is absolutely no reason for you to be here. It's a computer glitch."

Then Sue and I chatted for half an hour. First, we discussed my future work prospects before she turned the topic to general life conversation. I took an instant liking to Sue and we both enjoyed our chat very much. When she concluded our meeting, she apologised for the computer glitch, wished me well in my job search and indicated that she thought I wouldn't have trouble finding work. But I missed the twinkle in her eyes as I was to later discover that Sue had an idea quietly formulating that was directly connected to my future.

At 5.00 pm Sue left her office to meet her husband Tom for dinner at their favourite restaurant. Tom saw her running toward the restaurant and paused. She still took his breath away. The love he felt for her expanded in his chest.

Sue entered the restaurant and saw her husband sitting at their favourite table. He waved her over and she sat down, throwing him a dazzling smile. He grinned, his eyes twinkling at her. How he adored her. Sue put her coat on the back of the chair and sat near her amazing husband. A waiter approached and they requested a bottle of New Zealand Pinot Grigio. There was much to celebrate.

Once they were settled with a glass of wine, Tom asked Sue how her day was. She smiled and took a sip of wine before she casually told him she had found his new administration officer. "She is perfect for the job."

Tom grinned. He trusted his wife's wisdom and her truth and honesty.

"It's meant to be is all I can say," said Sue. "To be fair to everyone, I will send you five candidates and you will have to pick her out yourself. That's the best I can do." Her confident glow told

Tom that choosing the candidate she had in mind was not going to be a problem.

Two days later, I received a call to inform me that my resume had been put forward for the position of administration officer and I had been selected as one of five people to be interviewed. Excitement bubbled up and filled my heart to the brim. My interview was scheduled for 1.00 pm the following day. "What should I wear?" I pondered and decided on a crisp white shirt and a black skirt. An unusual feeling stirred inside me, a feeling that there was more to this job than I was aware of.

The next morning arrived and everything flowed like clockwork. Lorenzo, my youngest son was ready for school on schedule which meant we headed out the door on time. That in itself, was a miracle. He wished me well in my interview as he scrambled out of the car, casually throwing his backpack on his back. He turned around and gave me one of his adorable cheeky smiles. It melted my heart. Yes, it was going to be a fabulous day.

Upon my return home, I quickly showered and then opened my wardrobe. As I looked inside I had a strong feeling that I should wear something different so I chose my new Vera Wang pink and blue print top, a pair of plain black silk trousers and my new sling-back pumps. It was a tad dressy for an administration officer position but my inner knowing said, "It's more appropriate than you know." I felt confident as I walked out the door.

The hospital doors opened wide as I stepped inside and the smell of hospital-grade disinfectant hit my nose with full force. Yes, there it is. THAT SMELL! Indefinable, yet so strong. I reasoned it would kill every bug that crossed its path. Within a few moments, the smell became tolerable and I ventured toward the waiting room.

As usual I was ten minutes early for my interview so I could gather my feelings and thoughts. I spent a few minutes deep breathing to relax my body as I did not want to appear nervous. And I enjoyed the quiet moments as I went through interview scenarios in my head.

All to soon it was time to go in. I was greeted by a beautiful young blonde woman in her late twenties and an older, distinguished looking dark-haired man. They ushered me into the meeting room and the interview began. The man introduced himself as Tom, the CEO, and his colleague Mary, the office manager. To my amazement I was relaxed and comfortable in their presence. We looked at each other and smiled. In that moment, I realised that maybe this job was mine! After the usual pleasantries were concluded, I was asked the usual relevant questions. As I answered each one, Tom and Mary exchanged glances and nods of approval which helped me to relax even more until Tom raised what he believed could be a potential problem if he offered me the role. He believed I was over qualified for the job and was worried I would become bored.

Looking directly at Tom, I explained that I was completing other projects and that the position would suit me perfectly. He and Mary nodded to each other in a quiet way and the moment of panic was gone. Just before I left, Tom mentioned that while Mary was responsible for organising their fundraising events, I would be invited to attend if I wanted to assist in any way. He explained that the way I had dressed for the interview was perfect given that part of the role.

I left the office feeling positive that the job was mine, but a niggly thought pattern emerged that maybe I wasn't the person they were looking for. Sensibility and reason prevailed and I decided that if the job was mine I would be successful. If not, there would be a reason why and I would keep looking.

Three days later I received a call from Mary. She told me that the job was mine if I wanted it. I said yes, definitely, and thanked her. We discussed the necessary details and I put the phone down. Needless to say, I did my happy dance around the kitchen. Everything was moving forward for me. This job would prove to be the beginning of amazing experiences that would definitely assist my life purpose.

On his way home from work after concluding the last interview, Tom had gone over the five candidates in his mind. The job requirements were very specific. It was not just an administration officer position as the Research Foundation conducted fundraising events and everyone participated. In addition, they were a small team of four who worked closely together so it was imperative that everyone liked each other. But he was confident he had made the right decision.

Tom put his brief-case down in the hall and looked for Sue. He found her sitting in her favourite chair, snuggled in her pale-blue cashmere blanket and walked across the room and kissed her.

With a cheeky grin, she asked, "So, tell me, did you find her?"

He looked adoringly into her eyes. "Yes, my darling, that was the easy part. Tala is perfect for the job. We're going to offer it to her tomorrow. Our breakfast ladies are going to love her."

Sue smiled and said, "Yes they will."

Chapter 12

Breakfast at T's

I quickly settled into my new role as administration officer at the Research Foundation and enjoyed working with Mary and Tom. Mary was a confident young woman who oozed natural beauty and gentle femininity and Tom was nurturing and dedicated in his role as CEO. I often thought of him as the Silver Fox. He had a lovely personality and a charming smile. The ladies were very fond of him and he was the consummate professional and a true gentleman.

Within two weeks I was informed that the monthly breakfast fundraising event was approaching. Raising money for local medical research aligned with my need to be of service and it is such a worthwhile cause. The breakfast events were held in a beautiful function room at a popular five-star hotel situated directly across the road from the city's main seaport. With a magnificent mountain in full view, it encapsulated the backdrop of a picture-perfect postcard.

The hotel function room we used for the smaller monthly breakfast events seated two hundred guests. A set menu and a banquet of delicious pastries, tea, coffee and juice was offered and the camaraderie between us and the hotel staff was professional and friendly. I relished in my new-found confidence. To be part of organising such amazing events was a highlight of my job.

The five years I spent working at the Research Foundation were memorable. Setting up the function room for the monthly breakfast functions was the favourite part of my job. Each year, the four seasons would come and go and each season would present its own story. They also coincided with the four aspects of the Divine Union Relationship I was researching at the time.

Winter was my least favourite season. For three months, I would wake to the sound of the alarm buzzing in my ear. When I heard the alarm, inwardly, I knew it would be 4.30 am but I fervently wished it was not. The chilled air would whip around my ears as I pulled my dressing-gown closer and I knew the freezing cold outside would be even worse. My pre-ordered cab would arrive at 5.30 am so I could be at the hotel by 6.00 am to check off the guest list and make sure the tables were correctly set. I was fastidious in ensuring there were no lipstick smears left on the polished glasses and that the cutlery was sparkling clean.

As I carefully completed my tasks, a quiet reverie would fall over the room. With deliberate steps, I would walk around and re-check my work. Outside, pitch-black winter skies would reverently hold twinkling stars and a golden full moon shining her love on the world. Twinkling bright fairy lights would hit the sea and be reflected back against the floor-to-ceiling windows. It was like watching a fairy-book story come to life. Pearlescent light would move in a graceful dance and the table centrepieces looked dignified, creating a sense of beauty, a lovely feminine touch.

Within half an hour, the sun would peek above the horizon and the sky would be painted scarlet. The mountain top would glisten with crisp white snow and lower down, thick blankets of snow on the mountain shoulders conveyed strength and fortitude. She would echo her song of silence. I often wondered what secrets were hidden there. Aboriginal culture held her in great esteem. The sights were breathtaking, but the temperature outside was freezing and I was very happy to be inside, joyful and warm. By 6.45 am, we would be ready to greet our guests.

This first season, the first aspect of love, contains new beginnings and waiting. The deep, unknown void stirs the awakening of the Divine Union. All possibilities sit and wait in anticipation, but are yet to evolve. There is much to learn in this stage and patience sits at the fore. The feeling of divine love is overwhelming. The inner sanctuary of the heart opens to allow the connection to the Divine Union to begin. We are being encouraged to look beyond the limitations of physical beauty to discover the subliminal feelings that radiate in divine love. Be brave, or not, but romance is definitely in the air. The preparation has begun.

Spring time would open to a palette of pastel colours. Pink flowering blossoms would blanket the trees. Vibrant lush greenery would be seen in abundance in gardens everywhere. Flowers would begin to bloom. Heavy winter coats would be left at home and in their place, the ladies would wear light cotton coats and silk scarves in floral colours. The temperature would have risen enough for us to feel a lightness in our hearts and a spring in our steps.

This second season, the second aspect of love, brings hope and new ideas to the fore. It holds the hope that romance can deepen and be explored in deeper levels of intimacy and emotional connection. Clarity in love is being brought forward. The heart is feeling deeper feelings and the mind is thinking clearer thoughts. Perception is finally opening the heart to the outer door of the inner sanctum. The true beauty contained in love is available, but not always accessible. The heart has to be completely healed. Be brave, as the heart needs to stay open to allow divine love to enter.

Summer would present the full blistering heat of hot days and still hotter nights. Pretty dresses and slinky shoes would dazzle us. The room would be set as brilliant sunlight splashed on the windows, reflecting light as it bobbed on the sea. Golden sunbeams would frolic and tumble as light would dance on the tables with glee like children at play. Dreams and wishes would be shared between the attendees. Christmas time would be approaching and life would be busy as people gathered presents and gift ideas for loved ones and prepared for Christmas celebrations.

This third season, the third aspect of love, is the time of cementing ideas and finding true purpose and exploring the full implications of having a divine, healthy relationship. A balance of the connections of heart, body, soul and mind are being seen and the heart is brimming with light and purity. The puzzle pieces of the divine relationship are fitting into place. It is a time of tweaking patterns and beliefs and making sure the heart is fully healed. Confidence and a surety, as never before, are found here. The inner sanctum of the heart is known. Check for subtle patterns and inconsistent beliefs that may still exist.

Autumn would creep silently along the broad beam of time. Autumn is my favourite season of the year. We would often experience an Indian summer, when the days would be glorious and the sun still emitting ample warmth and the nights cool but not freezing cold. The ladies would layer their clothes and the latest fashion boots would be the norm. Sunlight would be draped across the water like layers of fine silk and the morning dew droplets would look like pearl earrings. Crisp golden orange leaves would leap and fly in the air and then effortlessly sway down to touch the ground. It was as if they knew their fall would be softened on impact. The ladies would sit in the warmth of the sun and enjoy each moment, not wanting to rush off to work. They would gather in groups to talk and stay a few extra moments but were unsure as to why they did so. They would speak in hushed tones, yet were excited that magic was definitely in the air!

This fourth season, the fourth aspect of love, is the most surprising of all. Letting go of the old conventional ways and bringing in the new divine path is the cornerstone of this aspect. We are being encouraged to keep focused and allow the Divine Union to begin. Believe that all things are possible. Freedom and wonderment feel like leaves falling to the ground. And we know that our landing will be soft as we bring into the world the beauty of divine love. It will seem as if a kingdom awaits you. This relationship kingdom consists of love, compatibility, laughter and joy, and being treated as an equal in all respects. Connection and love is easy. All the puzzle pieces of divine love fit together in perfect alignment. Now the heart is healed and fully engaged in the inner sanctum of the sacred heart. It is imperative to build the foundation of friendship first. Divine Union must have a strong base on which to build this sacred relationship.

Our breakfast attendees were politicians, doctors, researchers, scientists, business women and distinguished guests in the community. It was important to learn their names and to greet them accordingly. It was also important for me to stay in the background and offer assistance to Tom and Mary who organised and facilitated these events so effortlessly. They were professional and uplifting for everyone. Some breakfast attendees had been supporting the foundation for many years.

Tom's role as CEO was to secure guest speakers for our breakfast events. The guest speakers were a prestigious group of women who were leaders in their field. The one thing these amazing women had in common was their ability to inspire and uplift us to the extraordinary part of ourselves where true miracles live. Many of them had learnt to strive for excellence for themselves but also as an inspiration for others.

Chapter 13

Then I Saw His Face

Raising my four children, working two days a week and researching the Divine Union Relationship was the perfect work, life and family balance. I attended a support group on Monday nights, offering guidance to those who were struggling with love and life. Being of service gave me a greater sense of purpose. I kept learning as much as I could and the lovely people who attended this group were amazing teachers for me too.

This particular Monday night began like any other. Feeling tired after a busy weekend, honestly, I wanted to go home, have a cup of tea and go to bed. My inner knowing, however, had other ideas. I felt compelled to attend the support group. After an early dinner, I listened to that inner voice and headed out the door.

As the guest speaker that night talked about her difficult life experiences and how she had healed and turned her life around, I looked at the faces of the attendees and saw a look of recognition in each. Yes, life can be tricky to navigate at times. Thus, it is heartwarming to know that although we travel the same road called life, the paths we can take are unique; however, the ultimate destination remains the same.

Once the speaker had finished her inspiring talk, I ventured to the front of the room to commence our regular group discussion. As I put my book and pen on the front desk and settled back in my chair, I glanced around from left to right at the faces of the people sitting before me.

Suddenly, I noticed a man sitting in the third row on the left-hand side of the room. What happened next was shocking and exhilarating all at the same time. It felt like time and space suspended me in mid-air. Yes, that's very odd. Even for me. It was a very strange feeling.

Orchestrated by an unseen force our eyes met across the room. They locked in a stare of instant connection. In the next moment, it felt as if I had been pulled out of my body and I was standing just centimetres away from his face. I stopped breathing, but only for a moment.

Beautiful eyes, the colour of midnight coal twinkled at me in recognition and yet I knew I had never seen him until that moment. Long dark, almost black, hair spilled across his shoulders. It was perfectly straight. My eyes moved to study his face. He was breathtakingly handsome, beautiful even. "It's you, I know you." I said to myself inwardly. I just didn't know how I knew him in that moment. The shock of recognition hit my heart and I had to look away. I busied myself doodling a picture in my book, pretending that I was doing something very important. When I had the courage to look up again, he was gone. He had left the building!

A pain, a feeling of loss hit my heart with full force. Where did he go? Did I really want an answer to that question? I decided that I didn't and so I did what I do best, I ran away. I stopped attending the Monday night support group and I stayed away for a very long time. The connection and recognition I had felt toward the dark-haired handsome stranger had shattered me and I just didn't know what to do.

What had happened to me? Who was this man? Why did I feel so incredibly connected to him? The feelings I had felt about a complete stranger did not feel normal. That is, not normal in the sense that I'd never experienced this depth of connection. I had no answers to any of my questions.

My earlier experience with Dr John had been a platonic soul-mate experience. I knew first-hand what the soul-mate experience was. But the connection with this man, this stranger, was on another level entirely. It was an experience I was not ready to explore. Not yet!

Chapter 14

Facing the Truth

Three months passed before I was ready to return to the Monday night support group. My work at the Research Foundation was progressing well. It was liberating for me to love going to work and to be well-paid for doing what I loved to do.

For the remainder of each week I was content to continue my research into the Divine Union Relationship. My consultations with clients regarding their relationships were rewarding and I loved being a part of the process itself and being more connected to the people I was assisting.

Because I was so busy I had pushed the encounter with the stranger deeply into the recess of my subconscious mind. My intention was to not think about him. Of course, this wasn't facing my fears at all so I eventually decided to return to the support group.

I arrived early and found a chair in the front row. Songs were an integral part of this group and one of the counsellors had collated a play-list of popular songs. That night we sang an ABBA song called "I believe in angels" which is definitely one of my favourites. Who doesn't love an ABBA song?

The guest speaker had finished talking and I found myself once again at the front of the room, ready to participate in the group discussion. I placed my book and pen on the table and looked around at the people in front of me. Eyes, the colour of midnight coal were boring into mine. Wow, the dark-haired handsome stranger had returned! Fifty people were looking intently at me. It was my turn to speak.

Nervously, I stood up and gave a talk about the significance and importance of un-conditional love and the need to fully love and accept ourselves. Many people nodded in understanding and appreciation. As I sat down I peeked across the room. Those eyes, the colour of midnight coal were boring into mine. As much as I hated to admit it, I couldn't take my eyes off him either. What to do next? Behave normally. How was I supposed to do that? No idea. I really needed a drink of hot chocolate!

Chapter 15

Soul Sisters

Soul sisters are an integral part of a woman's life. They keep our sanity in check and add a different dimension of love in our lives that would otherwise be missing. Lilly and I had formed our soul bond when she was my student. She had a deep connection to crystals, she adored them. For seven years, she studied meditation and soul growth with me and during that time our connection strengthened. Lilly was my soul sister. She had a giving heart and a genuine desire to help others. We understood each other completely.

Lilly and I would often attend the Monday night support group together. After the group finished, our ritual was to visit a nearby all-night bakery, a place very popular with the tourists who visited our glorious paradise state. We would both order a hot chocolate and a scrumptious slice of cake, not bothering to count the calories we would consume. That is something we would worry about later.

Lilly became a confidante and I shared my life experiences with her. She knew about the pain I had endured in my past relationships and she knew about my soul-mate connection with Dr John. She also knew how much effort I had put into reassembling my life and applauded my courage and bravery. In addition, she understood that some of the struggles I had endured threatened to steal my peace of mind. And she knew that there were times when I wanted to give up but knew that I wouldn't. She knew it all! Lilly loved and supported my new path unconditionally and I was immensely grateful for her friendship and support. It meant the world to me.

When I shared my experience with the handsome stranger with Lilly, she encouraged me to find out more. "I am glad you've returned to the group," she said. "I'll help you through this. This man might be someone important, a future partner perhaps or he might have something to teach you. Either way, you need to keep going to the support group and find out." Lilly had that look in her eyes that suggested she was serious and that I should pay attention to her advice. She was right. I needed to know if the connection I felt with the handsome stranger was something important or if he had something to teach me about love.

As I have matured as a woman, I've realised, with a profound sense of wonder, that I still feel young inside. Sometimes, I walk through the house and catch a glimpse of myself in the mirror. Mother nature has been kind to me, and I haven't sustained too many wrinkles yet, but it's more than that. I still feel young at heart and I refuse to let age define me. My defiant, stubborn streak comes to the fore and I know that I love being a rebel. Just a little! I have no intention of being stuck in a box labelled "old age". Young at heart it is! It's true that sometimes I embarrass my children, but that's okay. They go with the flow now.

Lilly and I arranged to meet at the next Monday night support group. As I walked in the door a knot the size of a small mountain formed in my stomach. I arrived early so I could choose a seat near the front of the room. That way, I decided, I wouldn't have to look at the handsome stranger. It wasn't a mature way to proceed. I know what you're thinking, face him head on. Yes, that would be the sensible thing to do and is exactly what I would recommend to my clients. This is no ordinary man though. Trust me, you'll see.

Getting to know someone on an emotional, romantic level takes us into territory unknown. The sensation that's referred to as the 'falling' that happens when you're 'falling in love' is one of the most incredible experiences we can have. Our endorphins fly without fear, just like superwoman or superman. We believe we are invincible, that we can leap off emotional tall buildings and fly without an emotional parachute. Crazy thoughts like that were sifting through my mind as I sat and waited for the group to start. I really needed to calm down.

Love isn't age restrictive either. Don't let anyone tell you otherwise. I felt like an eighteen-year old girl again, just with a lot more life experience and wisdom. I thought that my past experiences with love would prepare me for what was happening. They didn't. I wasn't aware that the handsome stranger's presence would affect my heart, body, soul and mind so much. My nature is to be cool under pressure. He was a pressure cooker, bringing to the fore feelings, connection and emotions I had never felt before. What was going on here? I had no idea and determined it was best to proceed with caution.

Over the next two weeks, I planned a course of action. It sounded amazing inside my head. You know, the place where all the crazy thoughts live when you can't decide the best course of action to take. Yes, the ones that make no sense at all, only to you. In my wisdom, I decided to do nothing at all. I concluded that if he was interested, if the handsome stranger was remotely interested in me, then he would come over and talk to me. Decision made!

Many months later, one night after the support group, Lilly drove us to our favourite bakery and we sat in silence, deep in our own thoughts. She began to give me that stare. I knew what she was thinking. Because I was thinking the same thing. Something should have happened by now. What was going on? We sat down to have our hot chocolate and cake.

"Has he talked to you yet?" asked Lilly.

I shook my head.

Lilly stared at me for a long moment and finally said, "You are patient if nothing else."

I kept sipping my hot chocolate thinking that it was a huge mistake and that the connection between the handsome stranger and me was nothing at all. Perhaps it was just a figment of my over-active imagination?

When I suggested this to Lilly she surprised me by saying, "I've seen the way he looks at you and follows your every move. He doesn't take his eyes off you. It looks like a definite something to me. The way he looks at you isn't ordinary or just as a friend. It's smoking hot!"

I grinned. Lilly had such an exuberant way with words!

For months, I had been attending the Monday night support group but there was nothing to share. I had no news to tell Lilly. So, I made a decision. I decided to wait and let the handsome stranger talk to me. Yes, I felt it was important for him to find his way as a man and if he was interested he would talk to me. It's a well-known fact that if a man is interested in a woman, he will pursue her. If he was healing or not ready for a relationship, then he would hold back and take his time, retreat or do nothing at all. I knew that I could have approached him and that if I did so he would definitely talk to me. Yet I knew intuitively that this man was struggling with something very deep or painful and that I needed to let him be.

For months and months and months nothing happened. And in a strange way, I was relieved. Nothing happened at all. Except he kept staring at me. He would stare at me with an intensity that would make my heart skip a beat. I reasoned that eventually, he would talk to me if he wanted to. It was best not to think too much!

It's perfectly okay for a woman to ask a man out on a date. That's absolutely fine. The Divine Union, however, is a different dance of love. Allowing the man to take the first steps releases the seed of the Divine Union energy, a connection that is instinctive to his nature and is an important part of the divine love connection process. It's a way to make sure that you don't become involved in a conventional relationship. I knew that everything was going to be perfectly okay.

It was now getting close to Christmas time, that magical time of year. I love Christmas time and spending time with my family. Confusion was still paramount, but in slow increments, I gave up hope that the handsome stranger would ever talk to me. In fact, I stopped thinking about it and just let it all go.

Finally, one night at support group I was waiting for Lilly and I found myself standing next to the handsome stranger. He was so tall and so handsome. I looked into eyes the colour of midnight coal. Taking a deep breath, I smiled at him. It was the friendliest smile I could muster. He stared, no, he bored a look deeply into my soul. Then what he did next was totally unexpected. He returned my smile with a dazzling smile of his own and said nothing. Seriously?

He was so used to women falling over his every word that he didn't think about talking to me first. The handsome stranger had become complacent. He thought that I would make the first move and talk to him, just like all the other ladies did. He certainly had no shortage of ladies vying for his attention. Trust me.

But I stood my ground and just stayed close enough to feel his presence. Finally, in sheer exasperation I yelled in my head, "Dude, for goodness sake, just say hello, I won't bite you."

Time stood still for a moment and in slow motion he turned around to look at me as if he had heard every word I had said. He smiled. And then, as if it were the most natural thing in the world to do, he said, "Hello, it's lovely to finally meet you. I've been waiting for a very long time to talk to you."

Chapter 16

Loving Presence

As if by magic, the handsome stranger turned toward me, close enough that I could almost feel his breath. We began an amazing conversation and talked non-stop for the next fifteen minutes. It felt as if we were great friends who had just been re-acquainted after a long absence. It was easy, it was effortless. The connection between us was electrifying and people were looking at us, being pulled into the joy and laughter we were emitting. A glow, an indescribable feeling, filled the room. My lesson of patience had finally been learnt. I wondered what would happen next?

He told me his name was Matt, that he played the guitar and he loved to sing. A strong emotion stirred. It was that gooey feeling you get when someone tells you a precious secret that touches your heart. My heart swooned. My two favourite things in the whole world. Matt said that he would like to play the guitar and sing a song for me sometime and I was delighted. Lilly approached us saying it was time to go. She smiled at me. Our weekly trip to the bakery to chat was imminent.

Matt said, "Goodbye, I'll see you next week Tala."

I smiled and replied, "Definitely Matt, see you then." I loved the feeling of discovery contained in the play of new experiences and I wondered what would happen next.

Once Lilly and I arrived at the bakery we ordered our drinks and found a free table. Immediately, she asked for all the details and giggled when I told her I had yelled at him in my head.

"Only you would do something as unique as that Tala," she said.

I agreed and said that we would talk later as it was time to go home.

We made our way back to the car via a laneway and passed beautiful old sandstone buildings that were centuries old. They were a combination of history and new refurbishment which gave them an aura of mystique. Tourists loved visiting this part of the city. It provided a glimpse into the past about how difficult life would have been for the islanders in days gone by. Visitors also loved our crystal-blue waters, white sandy beaches and exploring the delights of our vast national parks.

The next morning, I woke early, incredulous that Matt had finally spoken to me. He had given me a strong indication that he wanted to get to know me better. I felt the same way so from the next Monday night we began to talk to each other. My intention was to take things slowly and see where our friendship would lead.

Conversation, laughter and immense joy filled the air when Matt and I were together. Lilly was thrilled and encouraged us to explore a friendship. It took Matt a while to feel comfortable enough to share his story with me. But I was in no hurry; I was happy to wait.

Slowly, I began to nurture my feminine side more. Without realising it, I had shut down that side of my nature. Matt was attentive and nurturing and I loved the warmth of his company and his appreciation of me as a woman. He was comfortable in his masculinity and we never ran out of topics to discuss. A few months later, Matt asked me out for a drink and shared his story.

We sat in a jazz bar and Matt asked me what I would like to drink. I asked for a white wine. I needed something to calm my nerves. As soon as we were settled, Matt began to talk. He told me that he was separated from his wife Greta. They had a daughter, Melinda who was sixteen years old. Their marriage had been fulfilling until seven years ago, Matt said, when he was involved in a motor bike accident. Until that time, he was self-employed as a psychiatrist and had a very successful private practice. His caring nature, warm personality and sharp intellect also helped create a successful family life.

Unfortunately, Matt sustained a brain injury in the accident and subsequently wasn't able to work. Memory loss made it impossible for him to do so. His wife Greta became the sole financial provider for their family. It was difficult for her to maintain her independence while caring for an invalid husband.

Finally, the difficulties they faced had become insurmountable and they had separated.

I was shocked and saddened that Matt had sustained such devastating injuries that had impacted his life on such a large scale. Now that I knew his story I understood more. Without knowing directly, I had already seen signs of his condition and now it made perfect sense to me.

Matt explained that he had died at the scene of the accident. His bike had hit an obstruction and spun out of control. He was flipped off the bike and hit his head. He told me that at the time of his death he saw a blinding white light and felt the presence of what could only be described as pure love. He revealed that he knew we were all loved by the presence of this love that was emanating from the blinding light. Until the accident, Matt had a scientific mind and a strong intellectual side.

What Matt saw and felt that day changed his life. He referred to his old way of life as "his limited understanding of life". The purity of love emanating from the light was not something his rational mind could comprehend at all. He was not a religious man either so he was happy that there wasn't a traditional choir of angels waiting to greet him. He told me if there had been, he might have thought it was all an illusion his mind had conjured up and that he wouldn't have understood what he saw and felt.

Matt said that the love he experienced when he died was truly indescribable. It was the way he said it and the incredibly deep soulful look in his eyes that startled me the most. He said, "We are supposed to love each other, to help one another, to encourage each other and to be more than we could possibly dream was even remotely possible." He also said that it was difficult to find the right words to express the love he felt and the things he saw.

By then, Matt was exhausted. We had been talking for three hours so we decided it was time to go home. When we walked outside, the twinkling stars beamed their brilliance from a clear, starlit night. I was humbled that Matt had trusted me, that he felt comfortable to share his story with me. Instinctively, I also knew there was more to the story yet to be told. But for me, at that point in time, it was enough.

Chapter 17

Guitar Man

It was now time for me to be brave, to walk along a path that didn't have a specific destination. All I knew for sure was that I wanted to spend more time with Matt. When I was in his company I felt joyous and happy. It was as if my feet didn't touch the ground.

I already knew that Matt wasn't ready for a long-term relationship. He was still in the process of healing from the breakdown of his marriage. For now, I was content to pursue a platonic friendship. It was easier for both of us. My heart had sufficiently healed but I was in no hurry to repeat the mistakes of the past. I was keen to learn what Matt was here to teach me and to find out, in time, if he was my Divine Union. At this stage I didn't have enough information to make a decision either way.

Meditation is my daily practice. Finding solace in the quiet, inner place was my saving grace during the early years of my recovery from a domestic violence relationship. I found that a quiet mind created inner peace and stillness and my day would be less troubled with the drama of everyday life's worries, concerns and problems. I wouldn't swap this daily practice for anything in the world. After I meditate, my inner self, or intuition as it's often called, allows greater clarity to prevail. The happy, fulfilled life I now lived was important to me.

Because meditation had helped me so much, I decided to teach others the principles and practices I had learnt and I began conducting eight-week courses with intervals in between to allow my students to apply the tools they had learned to their busy, everyday lives. My students indicated that when they incorporated meditation into their day, they felt a greater sense of peace and the ability to face problems or situations head-on. They also commented that they could sense a correlation between what they felt and what they thought, hence decision making was easier. This is called heart and mind cohesion and balance. My natural abilities as a teacher came to the fore and I loved teaching others how to improve their lives in a healthy way.

Matt mentioned that since his accident he had meditated regularly and asked if he could come along to a meditation class. I told him he was welcome as long as he didn't disrupt the group. Classes were usually well attended by women so when I told them the news, they greeted it with joy. A handsome man to talk to? Who wouldn't want to experience and savour that?

On a cold winter's evening in mid-July Matt walked through my lounge room door. Because he was so tall he needed to bow his head as he entered through the door frame. With ease and in silence he removed his shoes and made his way to a chair beside me. I smiled.

Twelve ladies took a deep breath in unison.

"Oh, my goodness," sighed Vivienne. "Tala, you didn't tell us that Matt was so handsome."

With a cheeky grin, I replied. "Vivienne, I really hadn't noticed."

Matt laughed out loud. He loved the attention. Vivienne gave me a stern look. She knew I wasn't blind. Many women who looked at Matt would definitely go weak in the knees. She was right, I did know how handsome he was, I just wasn't prepared to share my connection with him. The ladies settled down and the meditation class began.

Within a few short weeks it became clear that Matt and I shared a special connection, but I progressed in my usual professional, calm manner and refused to be drawn into complicated conversations with the other women. They were desperate to know if Matt and I were a couple. When I told them the truth, that Matt and I were platonic friends, they didn't accept that at all. Yet, it didn't stop them from vying for his attention with the hope of securing a date with him.

Little by little, I could see Matt blossoming. His life was still complicated with his ex-wife and daughter and they were still experiencing the pain of attempting to resolve feelings of hurt and abandonment. I was happy to be Matt's friend and to discuss his concerns but I wasn't prepared to become involved. Matt had to deal with his marriage issues first and I encouraged him to seek professional help. I knew it would help him to heal and assist him greatly.

That particular meditation class evolved past the eight-week time frame and we became a group of friends who gathered weekly to enjoy each other's company. Matt and I kept our friendship platonic. Soon, I was amazed to realise that eight months had passed by. The ladies in class encouraged Matt to play his guitar.

One of Matt's favourite musicians was Cat Stevens. He had listened to his music when he was attending college. Matt also started to write lyrics and would often fit his new lyrics to a popular melody. We were enthralled with Matt's gentle manner and warm sense of humour and his ability to encourage us to improve.

Getting used to Matt's frequent outbursts of energy and his ability to be spontaneous was startling. It was taking me time to get used to the way his mind worked. On one particular evening, he was telling me that he had bought new underwear and without hesitation, he pushed his trousers down to his thigh to reveal his fire-engine red cashmere underpants. Wow, I wasn't expecting that. I was so shocked that I grinned and I couldn't help noticing that he didn't have one ounce of un-wanted fat on him.

Oh, goodness me. I knew that I needed to get serious about getting fitter. I found it strange that Matt didn't notice that I needed to lose weight. In fact, he didn't judge my physical appearance at all and looked at me as if I were the most beautiful woman in the world. He reminded me of Mr Darcy in my favourite Bridget Jones movie. I was often taken aback by his reverent looks and the manner in which he treated me. Our connection was deep, soulful attraction and rock solid. It was devoid of judgement and the physical limitations of body perfection that we see in the media and popular magazines.

Matt continued to treat me with humble, elevated respect. Our main goal was to laugh and have fun, without complications, and just to experience a friendship that was innocent and pure. I felt confident that having a platonic relationship with Matt was important. We were able to purse a friendship and get to know each other without any added pressure. At this stage, I wasn't sure if I wanted to take it any further. I knew that Matt had resolved the painful ending of his marriage but he still needed to heal the pain that lingered in his heart. The last few weeks I had seen him staring at me with a lingering look and I knew that he definitely wanted to kiss me. Not yet, I decided. I still was not sure.

I was aware that if I let Matt kiss me, my sensibilities would be gone and I would open the romantic side of love with this beautiful, amazing, caring, sensitive man. That would be a disaster. Once I was involved, it would be nearly impossible to set myself free. I would be stuck in an unhealthy, unhealed relationship for a very long time.

My birthday arrived and I received cards and presents from family and friends and the usual good wishes from my Facebook community. They made me smile. There were fancy ecards and funny posts. I loved them. Matt had asked to see me on my birthday. He told me that he had a special treat for me. That was exciting. I couldn't wait to see what it was.

My youngest son Lorenzo was still living at home but he was now eighteen and independent. I loved the way our mother-son bond flowed easily. He is my youngest child, the baby of the family. When deciding on his name, I had no idea his name Lorenzo means "one who likes to drink alcohol". It is a fitting description for him and his friends as they explore, easing their way to manhood. Yes, Lorenzo is well-known for sport and his love of drinking a beer or two with his mates.

Matt had said he would arrive at my house at 11.00 am. That gives me plenty of time, I thought, as I headed to have my morning shower. It had taken me an hour to decide what to wear and I settled on a deep rose-pink top and silk pants which always made me feel feminine and special. Yes, perfect.

I was singing in the shower when I heard a loud knock on the bathroom door. Lorenzo yelled above my singing and the pounding of water in the shower, "Mum, there is a strange man at the front door. He has a guitar under his arm and he is carrying a bunch of bananas. Should I let him in or ask him to wait outside?"

Matt had arrived early having forgotten what time we had agreed to meet. Lorenzo was enjoying a quiet breakfast before going to college when he heard a thump on the front door. He opened it to find Matt standing there.

They locked eyes for a moment and Matt said with a wide grin, "I am here to see your mother. It's her birthday today and I have a special surprise for her. May I come in?"

Lorenzo returned his gaze with a look that said, "Seriously dude, you think I don't know that. She is my mother!"

Matt said, "My name is Matt, so tell me, who would you be?"

In response, Lorenzo turned away abruptly and left him standing outside the front door!

It took Lorenzo a few seconds to comprehend the man standing in the doorway. Matt was wearing a hat, a long coat and boots. He looked like Leopold from the movie Kate and Leopold, in which Leopold was a gentleman from an earlier era, with an otherworldly manner. Yes, that description fitted Matt perfectly.

I called out to Lorenzo, "Yes, let him in. His name is Matt and he's a friend of mine."

Lorenzo said, "Are you sure you want me to let him in? I could ask him to wait outside. I have to go to college and I need to leave now." It took a few minutes to convince Lorenzo that Matt was my friend and that it was fine to allow him to come inside. This was all very difficult to say the least. Being in the shower while this was transpiring wasn't helpful at all. However, it was all very funny and chaotic and confusing, very much like Matt, in fact, and it was a birthday I will never forget.

Reluctantly, Lorenzo said, "Okay, I'll ask him to wait in the lounge room." Lorenzo emphasised the words *lounge room* just to make sure that Matt understood he wasn't welcome in the bathroom. This wasn't what I wanted to be discussing with my eighteen-year-old son. I heard the front door close and then I heard the zip of the guitar case being pulled open. Ah, I thought to myself. Perhaps I am going to receive a special treat today.

I quietly opened the bathroom door and peered out into the lounge room to see Matt sitting on the couch quietly strumming his guitar. "Matt, I'm just getting dressed and I will join you soon."

When I walked into the lounge room, Matt stood up and reached down to give me a hug. "Happy birthday Tala," he exclaimed with enthusiasm. I seriously hoped he hadn't crushed one of my ribs. It was a very warm hug and I laughed out loud as he put me down. He looked at me with a loving look that nearly melted my heart and laughed as he told me he was so happy to see me.

Then, very proudly, Matt handed me a bunch of organic and very brown and unattractive bananas. I looked at them and felt a huge rush of excitement. I am allergic, really badly allergic to flowers and I usually panic whenever anyone unknowingly gives them to me. But Matt had remembered how much I love bananas. They are my favourite fruit. I eat them cold, I eat them hot, I adore them! The bananas he had bought me were organic, not sprayed with nasty chemicals and the colour was perfect. They were perfectly ripe.

We went into the kitchen and I asked Matt if he would like a cup of tea. He said yes, so I reached for my fine-bone china cups and teapot as I arranged a few bananas, soft cheese and other fruits on a platter. Matt gazed at me with a deep soulful look. Perhaps today was the day? Yes, he was going to kiss me, of this I was sure. I knew it in the depth of my heart. And then I panicked. I should have let him and he wanted me to, but something didn't feel right, even on my birthday, the day when dreams and wishes come true. Yes, I had feelings for Matt. They were real and pure and something else I couldn't quite define. But there was still something niggling inside me and very soon I would discover what that niggling feeling was.

I changed the subject and Matt and I began to talk. He looked at me, knowing I had avoided his kiss, yet unsure of why. I wasn't ready to talk to him about it so we pretended that it hadn't happened. Matt told me that I had a beautiful golden glow around me and that he always felt safe and protected when I was by his side. He had restored my faith in my ability to let a man close to me again. He had allowed me to feel the beauty of romantic love. Matt treated me like a beautiful woman. He was a treasure beyond words.

The moment was gone and Matt was his usual effervescent self once more. "Tala, come into the lounge room. I have a special treat for you. You are going to love this," he said. We made our way into the lounge room and I sat in the chair opposite him. He retrieved his guitar and began to play a melody that was unfamiliar to me. In a soft gentle voice, Matt sang and played me an original song he had written for my birthday. He wrote a birthday song just for me!

The melody was lyrical, pure and sweet and the words were about a woman who was beautiful, strong and caring. The lyrics told the story that she had started an amazing journey and met a man. It talked about her soul, her inner glow and her love for all things. Matt gave me a copy of the lyrics and I sang them with him. The words had come directly from his heart and soul and it was the most precious gift I could have received.

I realised, in that moment, what the niggling feeling had been. With sadness, I understood that Matt wasn't my Divine Union. He was an aspect, my Heart Soul connection. Matt and I were connected on the levels of heart, body and soul, but not the mind. I had developed feelings for Matt. We connected on a deep level and I was also physically attracted to him. But the mind connection was missing. This wasn't just because of the motorbike accident, although it was a factor. Mainly, we didn't think the same way about important life issues. I also believed that Matt needed therapy to heal the hurt and grief of losing his marriage. To love and be loved is the balance needed to sustain a healthy relationship. Matt needed to learn how to open himself up to receive love again.

He was still scared, holding a belief pattern that love was going to hurt him. Although he was content to offer his heart to me, he wasn't ready to receive love from me. He was unavailable. Our perspective and views about this were not in harmony

We had our special picnic and then it was time for Matt to leave. As we said goodbye Matt walked toward his car. I watched him exude a child-like innocence as he walked and yet I sensed he was carrying inner turmoil that gave him no inner peace. Matt was my first aspect of love in the Divine Union Relationship.

A few weeks later I attended a festival with Lilly. She was ready to commence her work in the area of health so I had offered to assist her. I was talking to a lady about the Divine Union Relationship when I heard a deep voice say, "I would like to book an appointment to have a Divine Union blueprint analysis with Tala." Lilly smiled at him and booked the appointment. He pointed to the sign on the wall and declared, "Divine Love, yes, I want that. That's exactly what I'm looking for."

I turned to look and was greeted by a tall, well-dressed man. "Hello, I'm Tala," I said. As I looked into deep honey-brown eyes I felt something familiar about this man. Here we go again! It was the same feeling I had felt when I met Matt, only this time it was stronger.

"Lovely to meet you Tala, I will see you soon," he said.

I remember thinking that I really did hope so. I wanted to meet this man again!

There was a distinct twinkle in those honey-brown eyes. As he walked away from me, I wanted to yell, "Come back, I want to talk to you, I need to know who you are." Unlike Matt, he couldn't hear me and so he walked away. I was definitely interested in getting to know this man.

Summary: Third Stage of Love – Mr Unavailable

Heart Soul – First aspect

Mr Unavailable: The third stage of love is called the Heart Soul connection and is the first aspect of love contained in the Divine Union Relationship. The four aspects of love feel exactly like the Divine Union Relationship and in the beginning, the aspect components connect at the level of heart, body, soul and mind. However, each aspect of love is missing one component that is eventually discovered. The connections for the first aspect are:

- ❖ Heart – connected to heart feelings and romantic love
- ❖ Body – connected to intimate and emotional attraction
- ❖ Soul – connected to the inner self, the real you

The first aspect of love is the seed stage of the Divine Union Relationship. At the seed stage, the soft stirrings of love start to blossom. The development of the soul is the indicator for each person. Those who meditate regularly and have taken steps to evolve the soul may feel the seed stage as intense and overwhelming. The intuition is heightened and it is recommended to build a solid basis of friendship first.

Matt was the first aspect of love. I felt sad and disappointed that he wasn't my Divine Union, but also relieved that I had trusted my intuition implicitly and kept our relationship platonic. I had a strong feeling that something was missing between me and Matt. It is imperative to trust your intuition and follow the promptings it gives you. For the Divine Union Relationship to become viable, two people must connect fully and completely at the four levels of heart, body, soul and mind.

Matt and I connected on the levels of heart, body and soul. This means that I had genuine heart emotional feelings for Matt and he had genuine feelings for me. We also connected on the soul level of connectedness, of feeling that we had known each other before as we could communicate by being real and honest with each other, our true selves. At the personality level, friendship was easy for us and we were very relaxed in each other's company.

A strong friendship is needed to create a solid foundation in the Divine Union Relationship. You need to have a solid platform on which to build a relationship. Matt and I were also physically and emotionally attracted to each other and I'm sure making love would have been amazing. However, the mind connection was missing for us.

The injuries Matt had sustained from the motorbike accident had definitely impacted on him and his life. But that wasn't the main reason he wasn't my Divine Union Relationship. The main reason was that we didn't think the same way about important things. Our perspective and views and values were not in harmony.

Matt believed that I should heal his heart and that if he loved me strongly and deeply enough that I would do so. Unfortunately, the heart doesn't heal that way. The heart has to be ready to receive love from another person. Matt needed to seek counselling and support to heal his heart. It was his responsibility alone to heal. I would have encouraged and supported Matt to do that every step of the way. Allowing another person to be responsible for themselves is the greatest gift we can bestow. Sadly, Matt and I were in different places in our lives. My healing experience with Dr John had accelerated my healing path and my heart was ready to have a healthy, committed relationship.

That precious moment, Matt's birthday gift, still fills my heart with love and gratitude. For this is the place where special gifts live. These are the rare, golden opportunities and experiences that life presents us with and this is the kind of magic that has the ability to change us forever. Something deeper opened up in my soul that day and I realised a very important fact. Matt had allowed me to see truth, honesty and purity in his heart and soul. He taught me that his truth, honesty and purity were a direct reflection of my own. It's the purity and beauty of the heart and soul that finally sets us free. It keeps us focused on the fact that we can and should have it all!

The Fourth Stage of Love
Twin Soul – Mr Upgrade

Marriage vows ended for he
Reality moves and now he breathes
Business savvy, yes is he
This man who works with grace and ease
Will he play those same old games?
If so, that would be a shame
Will he stand proud like a man?
Will he reach out and take her hand?
Or will he simply want an upgrade?
To hide his shadow-side this day
The twin is the mirror image recall
Quietly he walks toward the stall
He proclaims, "I know the truth of love divine"
It's hidden in the heart sublime
There's a deep connection, but how can it be?
A triangle arises and now there's unease

Two ladies in tow who will he chose?
There's a choice to me made, who will lose?
Only the purity of the heart can see
The path that leads to happiness for he
But what about his pain and woe?
Has it healed, or will he go?
Down the path and then upgrade
To fulfil desires his past love forbade
Young versus old that same old game
But that's an illusion, they're both the same
The goddess in both women is alive
They have no need to stress or strive
The future sits where love now stands
The Divine Union path she always commands
Answers come not to the fore
Only love can reach his core
Only love will see him through
He must decide, we say to you
Fret not, keep reading, don't be dismayed
Divine Union will always lead the way!

Chapter 18

New Heights

My friendship with Matt ended to allow us to both move on with our lives. He was still adamant he wanted to pursue a romantic relationship but, unfortunately, he wasn't prepared to seek counselling so we arrived at an impasse. The connection between us was too strong to keep a platonic friendship intact so we decided to go our separate ways. It was the best thing to do. I really missed him and the pull to return and throw caution to the wind was a constant reminder of the battle that arises between the head and heart. The easy option would be to follow my heart and worry about the consequences later. This option would have led to pain and suffering. A deep knowing prevailed. If I was serious about obtaining my Divine Union Relationship, then I needed to take the higher path to love NOW. It was important to hold onto my goal. In moments of rational thinking, I decided that it wasn't viable or emotionally healthy for me to keep hoping that if I waited long enough, Matt would seek the help and guidance he needed. Sometimes, connection and deep feelings are not enough. It would never be enough. I can, and should, have it all!

Keeping busy was the best course of action to take so I buried myself in my work. My Divine Union Relationship consultations had now progressed to the next level. My research added new information and depth to the guidance and direction I was able to give my clients. I found my niche and was happy with my work/ life balance. I continued my role at the Research Foundation and helped to organise the monthly breakfast functions. The months quickly flew by.

And soon, Christmas time loomed ahead. At the Research Foundation, we organised nine monthly breakfast functions and two major fundraising events each year. The first major event was the International Women's Day Breakfast and the second, the Christmas Breakfast. My first experience with one of our major functions, the Christmas Breakfast was imminent. The ballroom venue held over a thousand guests. At this stage I had no concept of what was involved, nor the volume or work it would require for its success but I was positive it would be an amazing event.

During my first year with the Research Foundation, I had been inspired by authors Kaz Cooke, Fiona McIntosh and Katherine Scholes. These amazing ladies were invited as guest speakers to our breakfast functions. I was so excited to meet authors of this calibre. In fact, I was in awe. I felt humbled and inspired as I listened to their stories and anecdotes about their life's journey. Their poignant messages were relayed to the guests attending. The core message encouraged and inspired us. I held onto every word.

During a lunch conversation with my friends, we decided that we needed a girl's weekend away. Shopping was definitely on the agenda. We also decided that we wanted to eat really delicious food and visit the theatre. A weekend trip to Melbourne would be perfect. It would be a quick visit to restore our energy before the arrival of the craziness of the festive season.

The trip to Melbourne was the first time I had flown in an airplane in twenty years. I was so excited by the thought of having fun that I hadn't thought about how I would react. During the early stages of my marriage I began having panic attacks. They varied in degree from mild to absolute terror and I would experience trouble breathing. During these times, it would have been so easy to think that a heart attack was imminent. It was very frightening. Now I was heading into new situations and circumstances I couldn't control. But more growth and change was happening.

Our Melbourne weekend get-away finally arrived. I waited patiently for my friend Sharon to pick me up. As usual, she arrived exactly on time and I put my bags in the back of the car and jumped into the front seat. We headed down the highway to the airport and talked about the trip ahead. Once we had booked in, we sat in the airport lounge and enjoyed a cup of tea before our departure. All too soon the flight attendant informed us that it was time to board.

We boarded the plane and quickly found our seats. When we had checked in I found, to my dismay, that I wasn't sitting next to Sharon. We were seated at opposite ends of the airplane. Sitting together would have helped to calm my nerves. There was no way to rectify the problem so I decided to make the best of what would be a stressful situation.

Our flight was due to arrive in Melbourne in an hour and

fifteen minutes so it was a quick flight. Thank goodness! The roar of the engines filled the cabin and before I knew it we were hurtling down the runway at an extraordinary speed. Panic set in and then went into overdrive as I felt my stomach lurch. It was letting me know that the wheels were no longer touching the ground.

The plane soared into the clouds in what seemed like record time. It was normal speed but my heightened senses made me feel like everything was out of control. I kept reminding myself to breathe and I used the calming techniques my counsellor had taught me. For a moment, panic overwhelmed me and I wanted to jump out of the plane. Thankfully, sensibility prevailed and I realised that this wasn't a viable option. Firstly, I didn't have a parachute and secondly, I had a fear of heights. I told myself to keep breathing, just one breath at a time and all would be well. Eventually! I kept doing that and before I knew it, the cabin crew were offering passengers much-needed refreshments. A cup of tea always makes me feel better. It's amazing what the mind is capable of imagining. It worked and I was distracted for some time but that deep, foreboding feeling wouldn't leave me alone.

Just when I thought my nerves were slightly under control the very enthusiastic captain told us with a very cheery voice that we were travelling at 40,000 feet in the air. What! In my mind, there were too many zeros in that number. I then contemplated how awful it would be if the plane fell out of the sky. "Stop that nonsense," said my sane voice. "The plane is staying in the air; you have important work to do and people to assist with their life purpose." Momentarily, I wondered if my nerves would snap and then as if by magic or perfect timing, the captain urged the flight crew to prepare for landing. Finally, I would be able to get off this plane!

The thump of tyres hitting the ground pushed me back in my seat. They screeched as the plane pelted down the runway and then slowed down until the engines stopped. By this stage, I felt as if the weight of the world had been lifted off my shoulders. Wow, I had survived the flight but I felt nauseous and drained beyond belief. I wasn't aware at this stage that I would travel on planes extensively during the next phase of my life and that I would learn to enjoy flying and feel more comfortable in the air. Within ten minutes we were headed through the terminal to collect our luggage.

I found my friends Sharon and Shirley amongst the throng of passengers and decided that our first task upon leaving the airport was to find a restaurant. Amazing food was exactly what I needed to settle the nerves in my stomach. We entered a lovely restaurant, found a table and leisurely browsed through the menu selections. The food was varied and delicious.

Melbourne is a cultural city, a dynamic hub of activity and amazing food. It's also a very busy city with masses of people milling around like busy bees swarming from place to place. After a delicious lunch of burnt butter gnocchi and a drink of lemon, lime and bitters, shopping was next on the agenda. I was conscious that the Christmas Breakfast event was approaching so it was the perfect time to buy something new to wear.

We scoured the shops for hours trying on outfits and shoes. It was heavenly to spend time with my friends. We gazed at some of the beautiful fashions on display. Within a couple of hours, we were laden with bags of beautiful clothes to take home with us.

The rest of our weekend was spent eating and exploring Melbourne. We visited side-alley cafes that served amazing food.

The weekend was a gateway to total indulgence. But all too soon it came to an end and it was time to catch our flight home.

The return flight was slightly better as I now knew what to expect. This time, I put my earphones in, started my portable disc player and allowed the soothing music to settle my nerves. Within ten minutes the crew were offering drinks. I ordered my usual cup of tea and sat back thinking about the weekend and how liberating it was to begin travelling. That trip to Melbourne was the beginning of my future travels.

Chapter 19

Helping Hand

The hospital CEO often invited Tom to attend lectures given by the research grant recipients and on one particular occasion he asked if I would like to accompany him. Curious about the lecture, I accepted. We set off together on a warm summer's day. Unbeknown to me I would learn something very important that would affect great change in my life.

Tom and I arrived at the lecture promptly and took our seats near the front of the auditorium. A gentleman, perhaps in his late thirties, strode onto the stage. He turned to look at the audience and smiled as he sat down on the stool provided. His face was slightly flushed but his eyes conveyed a look of determination and also a glint of knowing that he was about the share important information with everyone present.

The medical researcher began to speak in a clear, crisp voice. He beamed with confidence and surety. The purpose of his lecture was to impart knowledge about visceral fat and how it plays a vital role in ill-health. The young man began to share the findings of his research. With gentleness and kindness, he told us that if we have a large, fat stomach the visceral fat contained there would release harmful toxins into our bloodstream. The fat affects our organs, he stated, especially the heart and liver. Insisting that he wasn't being unkind, he was also definite in conveying that he didn't consider a woman unattractive if she was carrying extra weight. He also said that men carry weight in the stomach as well so he wasn't being gender biased. This lovely gentle man told us very deep truths that were vital to our health and well-being. My mind began to race. I had much to think about. The lecture concluded an hour later.

Tom and I walked back to the office in silence, both deep in our own thoughts. I kept thinking about the weight I had gained during my marriage and still carried. Because I was deeply unhappy, at the time, I believed that my weight was the only thing I had control of. My husband abhorred larger women so I had stayed overweight to ensure he didn't want sex. But I wasn't married to him anymore and although I had trimmed down, I still needed to shift more weight.

After attending the lecture, I concluded that it was time to let the weight go and become the healthiest, best version of myself. As we neared the office, Tom looked at me with a very kind, almost fatherly expression and said, "How do you feel about the lecture Tala?"

Without hesitation, I replied, "Tom, the lecture was informative and really helpful. I now see how important health and vitality is to living a long, healthy life."

Tom smiled and walked into his office.

With renewed vigour and effort, I began to formulate a healthy lifestyle plan. It was best not to include the word diet, I decided. For me, dieting conjured feelings of lack and restriction. My plan included creating a healthy lifestyle that emphasised healthy eating choices and exercise. Strenuous activity wasn't going to be helpful due to past injuries I had sustained in three car accidents. My plan was simple and easy.

The elimination of sugar was imperative. My love affair with white sugar had begun a long time ago. Sugar cravings reverted me back to my childhood. In the mid-sixties, I was seven years old. Due to wartime restrictions and lack of finances, my mother gave me white bread covered in thick creamy butter and white sugar to eat as an after-school treat. She wasn't trying to hurt me, with severe monetary restrictions, she did the best she could with the limited resources she had. As a widowed mother, with thirteen children to care for I'm surprised we had any food to eat at all!

Some of her favourite recipes were short-bread biscuits and cookies laden with rich golden syrup. The more golden syrup she added, the more deliciously sweet they were.

My other favourite thing to eat as a child were butterfly cakes laden with jelly and cream, sprinkled with multi-coloured hundreds and thousands sugar crystals. Much to my mother's concern I didn't eat many vegetables when I was growing up. The only vegetables I ate were mashed and baked potato and mint peas. There was not much sustenance there and definitely not the vitamins and minerals I needed to thrive or the variety of good food required to sustain gut health.

I returned to work the following week and let Tom and Mary know that I was going to start a health programme. They were encouraging and committed to helping me stay on track. Their concern touched me deeply and I was moved by their desire to assist me.

With determined effort, I had decided that total elimination of sugar was my best course of action. So, of course my body went into shock and had a meltdown. I had a stomach upset for five days, followed by a terrible rash on my face as toxins began seeping out of my body. Progress? I felt sick, tired and during the first week I thought I had done the wrong thing.

Slowly, within a week I started to feel a little lighter. Within two weeks I felt considerably better and clearer in my mind. Within two months I felt amazing with more energy and stamina than I'd had in a long time. Within six months I had shed weight and was wearing clothes three sizes smaller. Slowly, I regained a womanly shape that I was very happy with. I didn't need the figure of a model to feel happy and confident. Being happy and content with our bodies will always be the best healthy version.

Finally, the week of the Christmas Breakfast arrived. The invitations had been mailed six weeks earlier and bookings were filled to capacity for one thousand, one hundred guests. The colour theme was festive red, green and white. Mary worked tirelessly, organising every last detail to perfection. I reconciled payments and helped to organise the gift bags for our guests.

The Christmas Breakfast needed to be set up the day before,

including ninety tables. All team members pitched in, accompanied by our trusted volunteers whose assistance was invaluable.

The wonderment I felt the first time I walked into the ballroom is still etched in my mind today. I walked in and quickly turned around and walked out, daunted by the massive room with its ninety tables. Then I took a large breath, calmed my nerves and took the lift to the ground floor to the downstairs café. It was only 10.00 am but I seriously needed a cup of tea. We had a lot of work to accomplish and I knew the time would fly by quickly.

During the next seven hours, together with our amazing volunteers we accomplished an incredible feat and we were delighted with the transformation. The ballroom looked amazing, decorated perfectly, bursting with festive cheer.

Sponsor's banners lined the main stage, along with large helium balloons. Crisp white tablecloths covered tables adorned with red and white centrepieces, green place cards and red trimmings galore. The magic of Christmas definitely filled the air.

Exhausted but happy we finished by six o'clock. It was time for an early dinner and to prepare for the next day. We all said goodbye and went our separate ways. As I walked out the ballroom door, I couldn't help but take a quick look behind me. The ballroom really did look spectacular. It was going to be an amazing day for our breakfast attendees.

After dinner, I retrieved the outfit I had bought in Melbourne, black silk Vera Wang trousers and a layered apricot silk shirt. The sleeves were cuffed at the wrist and free-flowing at the top like butterfly wings. I tried it on to make sure it looked right. As

I twirled around I concluded that I looked and felt very feminine and appropriately dressed for our special function.

All too soon the next morning arrived and I dressed quickly. It was a very special day. The cab driver phoned, letting me know he was outside. It was time to go. I applied a light smear of lipstick and headed out the door, excitement swirling at full capacity. Within ten minutes we had arrived at the hotel. I smiled. The morning was ready to begin!

Walking quickly, I entered the foyer of the hotel and took a lift to the second floor. As the lift came to a halt, I was greeted by the choir singing one of my favourite Christmas carols. The beautiful melody of 'Silent Night' created chills around my arms. This carol has special memories for me and I walked toward the men and women who were singing this beautiful song. Memories of my children as young ones excited about the Christmas holidays sprang to mind and my eyes misted over with tears of love. The singers followed with 'We wish you a Merry Christmas' and I knew our guests would be arriving soon.

Joy bubbled up inside me as I stepped once more into the ballroom. Yes, the room looked spectacular. I placed my bag near my chair and walked outside to join our team in the foyer. We wished each other good morning and Mary asked me how I was going. I answered that I was excited and looking forward to being part of the team. The hotel staff were buzzing around checking last minute details and looking impeccable in their black suits, white shirts and gloves.

It was time to greet our guests. Our small monthly breakfast functions hadn't prepared me for the enormity of the crowds of people who walked through the doors. Hundreds of people started heading up the stairs. Eight of us were standing together outside the ballroom handing out lucky door tickets and helping attendees find their tables. Momentarily, the scene was bedlam.

As attendees greeted me with a cheery good morning, I could hear their reactions to the stunning scene in the ballroom. "Oh, wow. It looks grand and so beautiful," they commented. I had to agree. Within half an hour all of our guests were seated and we were ready to begin. Tom beamed at me with a relaxed smile and as the Master of Ceremonies he headed toward the stage to formally welcome our guests.

Mary, Natalie and I were seated on the right-side of the room. This enabled us to stay in the background and allowed the function to progress with as little interference as possible. Tom welcomed politicians, distinguished guests and attendees. With the formalities over the breakfast began. Tom continued to share information regarding research programs and grant recipients and then introduced the main guest speaker.

Maggie Beer, well-renowned chef and television personality was our guest speaker. I found her to be absolutely charming. Maggie shared with us her personal life stories and her passion for assisting others. Her love of family and of her home in South Australia was evident. And, of course, her love and passion for cooking. Growing amazing produce is important to her. I remember feeling a sense of love from her that radiated around the room. Maggie Beer is a warm, special down-to-earth woman with the special ability to see into people's hearts. Everyone felt uplifted and inspired by this amazing woman. She also has a wonderful sense of humour and a depth of character that was heart-warming to see. It was my privilege to meet her.

Finally, it was time for fun and the lucky door and raffle prizes were given out. Our attendees were very supportive in donating money to medical research and we found that our fundraising efforts were productive. To date, seven million dollars has been raised and real headway has been made in the area of medical research.

After much frivolity and laughter, Tom gave away some amazing prizes ranging from pamper packs and jewellery to airfares and accommodation to an island destination. The winners were very happy with their prizes. Finally, the breakfast function was concluded. It was deemed an amazing success and many people later emailed Tom expressing their genuine thanks and gratitude to everyone involved.

The next ten days flew by. The festive season was upon us and my holidays would begin. I had planned to visit my family to relax, unwind, soak up the sun and flow with the experiences that would unfold next!

Chapter 20

Rainforest

Christmas celebrations and much-needed family time arrived. It was hectic but I enjoyed the time we all spent together. I had taken annual leave, allowing me four weeks to relax and capture the warmth of the sun. This long break was a deliberate move to take time to rejuvenate. I had grown considerably as a person and looking for love wasn't on my agenda but sometimes life has a different plan percolating quietly when we least expect it.

Lilly and I had decided to take a five-day trip to Byron Bay in New South Wales. Well known for its beautiful beaches, rainforests and relaxed lifestyle, Byron Bay sounded like the perfect holiday destination. We researched on the internet and discovered that the local Arakwai aboriginal people's name for the area is Cavvanbah, meaning "meeting place" and Lieutenant James Cook named Cape Byron after Naval Officer John Byron, circumnavigator of the world and grandfather of the poet Lord Byron. An amazing tourist destination and a playground for backpackers and international guests alike, it has a humid subtropical climate with hot summers and mild winters. Hot summers? Yes, December and January are the hottest months of the year. What were we thinking?

Lilly had met international best-selling author Blake Bauer at a mid-winter Melbourne festival where he was promoting his new book titled *You Were Not Born to Suffer*. They chatted as he signed a copy of his book for Lilly. Blake is a wisdom teacher and he mentioned he would be conducting a three-day workshop in Byron Bay and gave her the details. Lilly and I met and discussed details of the workshop later that day. It was unanimous. We decided to attend the workshop. As we booked our tickets we reasoned that the workshop would be interesting and helpful in beginning the journey to shift our limiting patterns and beliefs. I had an inner knowing that this retreat was going to be incredibly helpful.

On the 3rd January, Lilly and I headed to the airport on route to Byron Bay. We had packed light cotton clothes and a few silk shirts and Lilly packed dresses for evening wear, preparing for hot and very humid weather. We had booked a direct flight to the Gold Coast and a hire car to drive to Byron Bay. With my fear of flying still running high, Lilly sat next to me, allowing me to sit in the exit row. My nerves calmed down.

As the plane soared swiftly into the air I felt the same degree of uncertainty and discomfort as on my previous flight. Noticing my white-knuckled grip on the armrest, Lilly distracted me with conversation until the cabin crew offered us light refreshments. I enjoyed a cup of tea and we chatted some more. All too soon the captain was requesting the cabin crew to prepare for landing.

"Wow, where has the time gone?" I asked Lilly.

She smiled. "Time flies when you're having fun!"

"It certainly does," I replied.

After landing we collected our luggage and walked to the car rental reception desk. Lilly had chosen a brand-new SUV, a comfortable drive for the trip to Byron Bay. We put our luggage in the back seat, Lilly turned the music on and we settled in for the hour and a half drive down the Pacific Highway.

Lush vegetation and deep green trees were startling to our eyes. We couldn't believe how lush and vibrant the countryside was. Music filtered within the space around us. The quick beat of Café del Mar and the sultry swing sounds increased our already happy mood. It was a scene befitting any beach party. We were having fun, enjoying the happy vibe.

Finally, we arrived in Byron Bay and found our accommodation. It's amazing how inconsistent the accuracy of brochure photos can be. The pictures in the brochure highlighted a stunning beach scene with waves crashing on the sand. I couldn't wait to take my shoes off and walk along the beach to immerse myself in the crystal blue waters. Much to my surprise, as we rounded the bend in the road we found ourselves going further and further into lush tall, green trees. Wow! We arrived in middle of a rainforest.

Since I was a child I have had a morbid fear of being surrounded by trees. Camping or glamping isn't a pastime I have ever experienced for the simple reason that I'm not comfortable in forests. Lilly on the other hand, loved it immensely. As we peered out the window we saw the wooden cabin that was to be our home for the next five days. I took a deep breath and tried to relax. We couldn't change the booking so I was going to have to make the best of a stressful situation.

As I opened the car door, the heat and humidity hit me in the chest. It was unbearably hot and sticky. We gathered our bags and made our way to the reception desk to collect the cabin keys.

Lilly was thrilled. "Oh Tala, look at how beautiful it is here."

I smiled and nodded, not saying anything as I tried to hide my fear. It felt like the trees were so close that I was being suffocated.

After a friendly chat with the accommodation owners we headed to our cabin. They had explained that Byron Bay was experiencing a freak heat-wave, the worst it had seen in years.

"Of course, it is," I reasoned to myself. How would I learn anything of significance if life was normal?

Lilly opened the door and to my surprise the cabin was spacious and very clean. Beams of sunlight peered through the trees and were bouncing off the floor giving the room a sense of mystery and wonder. I was mesmerised by the patterns they were creating. Whenever we travelled, Lilly always allowed me to choose the double or queen size beds due to lower back trauma I sustained years ago. I am extremely grateful that she did so.

I put my bag near the queen-sized bed and looked up. There was a floor to ceiling window facing me and in the middle of the window was an enormous tree. Startled, I took a few steps back to get my bearings. It appeared as if the tree was standing inside the room, inside my bed. My mind couldn't comprehend what I was seeing I knew it was an illusion, that the tree was nestled in the rainforest. Its roots snuggled in the depth of the earth surrounded, cradled and supported by rich deep soil. But, momentarily, I stood there, totally transfixed. Interrupting my reverie, Lilly suggested we go into the township and find a restaurant for an early dinner. I quickly agreed and we headed out the door.

The main township of Byron Bay is located around a few street blocks. It made finding our way around relatively easy. When we came across a Hogs Breath Café, we decided that chicken, salad and curly chips were just what we needed. We enjoyed our dinner immensely. The staff were super friendly and the food was delicious and afterwards I suggested we go to the beach. Lilly agreed and we walked along the streets and peered into the various craft, clothing and tourist stores along the way. There was so much to see and do.

The waves crashing on the beach were magic and music to my ears. I adore the beach. I love sitting on the sand, going into the depth of silence and being immersed in the wonder of its simplicity and grandeur. Lilly and I took our shoes off and began to walk, falling into deep pockets of silky smooth white sand. The luxurious feel of the sand between my toes was delightful and we began a long trek to the other end of the beach.

As we neared the end of the beach we heard the sound of booming, pounding drums. I was smiling and Lilly knew how much I loved music. It was dark by that time and the lights from the streets twinkled and glowed as if they knew it was important to shine the light to reveal the path ahead. We could see people dancing, singing and swaying to the rhythm, allowing the beat to take them on a journey of freedom and fun. Small toddlers were showing bare bottoms, carefree, squealing in delight as their parents chased after them to put their clothes on. It was a beach party. It was absolutely magical to participate. Lilly and I joined the party and had an amazing time. Two hours later we decided it was time to go back to our cabin as we needed a good night's sleep. Tomorrow was going to be an interesting day!

Chapter 21

Healing Retreat

Lilly and I woke the next morning to the sound of birds chirping with animated delight. We enjoyed a leisurely breakfast, got dressed, gathered writing materials and a bottle of water and headed out the door. We were both excited about the course material and meeting new people.

The workshop retreat was scheduled for three days and would consist of intensive learning, sharing our life stories and eating healthy food. On the second night, I would experience a magical event that I would never forget. But more about that later. Approximately fifty people were attending the workshop retreat and it was lovely to see so many couples prepared to work on themselves and to strengthen their relationships.

The retreat venue was called Temple Byron. The temple was a

Yurt, a circular building with chairs and cushions and Blake's staff encouraged us to make ourselves comfortable as we settled in for the next three days. As I sipped peppermint tea, the gong tolled indicating it was time to begin the first day.

I found a chair on the left-hand side of the room, adjacent to where Blake was sitting. It felt like the right place for me and Lilly chose to sit next to me. Moral support was definitely on her mind, but at this stage she didn't know why. The session began. As is customary in group gatherings, each person in turn, introduced themselves and revealed why they were attending the workshop. Each member shared important information about themselves and we slowly began the process of interacting with each other. I said that I felt drawn to the workshop but wasn't sure why. Some people sitting near me, nodded in agreement and understanding. I added that I was sure it would become clear before the workshop ended. The morning passed quickly and lunch-time approached.

The kitchen and amenities were situated across from the temple. We found, to our delight, that the staff had provided trays of amazing hot vegetarian food. It was a sumptuous banquet! Lilly and I selected our food and made our way to a table near a beautiful weeping-willow tree that provided shade from the heat and humidity. Wow, the day was extremely humid, hot and sticky. My clothes were pressed against my skin as if trying to escape from the heat. As we enjoyed our delicious food, Lilly and I and chatted and then made our way back to the temple for the afternoon session.

Blake began teaching the depth of his wisdom and I was impressed with his heart-centred knowledge and compassion. As usual, I sat back and allowed others to share their stories and the problems they were facing. For many years, I had been travelling the path of healing and gathering wisdom on how to live a loving, happy and productive life. While I was aware that my healing wasn't fully completed, I had come to a place of happiness and peace. Perhaps I was here at the retreat to help others. This was only part of the truth, but I wasn't aware of that, not yet!

Later that afternoon Blake announced he had a lovely surprise for us. "Wow, that's exciting," I thought. I absolutely love surprises. We were told to make our way to the large room near the kitchen and take our shoes off. Hmm! I wondered what he had in mind? And was his idea of a lovely surprise the same as mine?

We all stood around the room, eagerly anticipating the joy of the surprise that was promised. Blake then grinned as he explained that we were going to do a Chi Gong session. Chi Gong actually means "life energy cultivation" and has its roots in Chinese medicine. It helps to develop human potential according to philosophy. Chi Gong involves co-ordinating slow movements, deep breathing and a calm state of mind. Easy? NO!

Lilly grinned at me. She was proficient in Tai Chi, a similar practice of Chinese medicine, and Chi Gong was going to be a wonderful experience for her. However, I was not feeling very confident at all. Initially, I didn't want to join in the session but I thought that perhaps I should participate and see what happened. How hard could it be?

To my surprise and delight, I found that the movement and energy of Chi Gong was slow, easy and steady. Halfway through the exercises they became a little more challenging but to my delight I was able to keep up with Blake. As I watched the faces of group members, I started to see a slight shift in expression, a change that indicated something deep and profound was shifting and moving within them. Somehow, something had slowly shifted inside me too. I couldn't say what it was. I felt free of something that had been sitting within my cellular memory for as long as I could remember. I had stored the memory in my subconscious mind. The session came to an end and I quickly brushed away the profound experience that had just occurred.

We returned to the temple after consuming more beautiful food and were ready for the final session of the first day. Blake asked us to take out our workbooks and complete the exercises. After an hour of writing down our thoughts and feelings we were encouraged to share them. Much laughter, merriment and a few tears surfaced as people began to share their life experiences and stories with the group. Blake gave each person the value and service of his wisdom with unconditional love and acceptance. It was a blessing to be part of this group.

With the first day concluded, we all said goodnight. We all agreed that the first day of the workshop had been amazing and we were excited to see what would transpire on the second day.

As Lilly and I made our way to dinner that evening we talked about the day's events. She asked me how I was feeling after the Chi Gong session. I shared what I had seen within the group and she confirmed that she had witnessed the same thing with her previous Tai Chi class. I also commented that it was interesting to be able to support those who were shifting limiting patterns and out-dated beliefs in their relationships and life choices. For me, it was humbling to be of service, to be part of something bigger than myself. I had spent many years on the path of releasing old patterns, beliefs and deep wounds. Ignorance is bliss, so they say. However, that isn't always true. The next few days would prove to be very enlightening!

During the night, I woke with a searing pain in my stomach. I moved across to my left side and found that my body hurt everywhere. Startled, I slowly sat up in bed. Why I was in so much pain? Chi Gong! I had used every muscle in my body in such a gentle way that I had forgotten that I was using muscles that I hadn't used for a while. Ouch!

Lilly woke and asked, "Are you alright?"

"No, I'm not. I don't think my muscles like Chi Gong," I replied.

We both started laughing at the ridiculous tone in my voice until I urged her to stop. Laughing wasn't helping the pain at all. Lilly handed me two pain-relief tablets with a glass of water and urged me to take them so I would get a restful night's sleep. Within half an hour the pain subsided and I fell into a dreamless sleep.

I woke the next morning still feeling sore but not the severity of pain I had experienced during the night.

As Lilly and I headed out the door, I looked at her for a moment and said, "Lilly, do you think Blake will encourage us to do Chi Gong again today?"

"Yes Tala, he definitely will," she replied as she walked toward the car.

I grimaced and I knew she was grinning, I just knew it!

The second day commenced and Blake said he had another surprise! I grimaced, refusing to look at Lilly. She was still grinning. He announced that Sacred Earth, my favourite group, were going to perform that night. Now, that was an amazing surprise. Blake and I were back on the same page! Prem and Jethro Williams are amazing. Their music is soulful, honest and pure. What a perfect surprise.

It was difficult to concentrate on teachings for the rest of the day but I managed to complete the exercises and the day evolved effortlessly. More people were shifting limiting patterns and out-dated beliefs. Blake was providing unconditional support, patience and acceptance as they began to see how their lives and relationships could be improved. The Chi Gong session was scheduled for after lunch. For a few minutes, I sat on the grass near the willow tree and deliberated if I should go. I decided to tackle the session and found to my delight that I was able to complete it without too much difficulty. Perhaps the sudden kick of adrenaline had something to do with the fact that Prem and Jethro were going to share sacred space and heavenly music with us. Definitely!

After a light dinner, Lilly and I returned to the temple for the Sacred Earth concert. Other retreat attendees had also arrived early to make sure they too would secure a good seat. We all sat together in the kitchen chatting about the concert when I realised I had left my bottle of water in the temple at the end of the day's session.

Ever so quietly, I entered the temple and found Prem setting up the sound system. A little awestruck, I wasn't sure how to proceed so I smiled and said a quiet hello to her. She returned my smile and said hello. My heart melted, just a little. Her voice is unique, so pure. It's as if angels have direct connection to her vocal chords. I found myself smiling, feeling bliss in my heart. Prem is beautiful in an angelic way. Her long dark hair, soft beautiful face and luminous eyes create a picture of womanly beauty. Her eyes hold the secrets of times long ago.

During the past few years I had been learning to see the beauty in all women and men. This can be confronting at times. Years of conditioning create a limited lens in the way we view the world we live in. Being young and having a slender body is considered perfection by our society's standards but as I grow in deeper understanding I am beginning to see and value that beauty is packaged in various shapes, sizes and ages. Love, that is, divine love isn't defined by age, shape or size. Our true being, our inner sacred heart, is the beauty that shines forth to capture the attention of the Divine Man or Divine Woman. It's a fact. Much to my surprise, it has been by my own personal experience and the experience of the many people I have consulted for.

It was 6.50 pm and Blake announced that Sacred Earth would begin the concert soon. We waited in anticipation as we readied ourselves for a wonderful evening. The room had been transformed with sheaths of silk and satin. Coloured candles swayed in the slight breeze that was wafting through the fabric walls of the temple. At the front of the room, Jethro was organising his musical instruments and Prem was sitting near the keyboard.

Blake introduced Sacred Earth and we gave them a warm welcome. We were ready to hear the wonderful gift of their beautiful music and we didn't have to wait too long. The haunting sound of a pan flute and Prem's voice broke through the silence. It seemed as if the silence was captivated by the beauty of a voice that required honour and respect. The purity of her voice reverberated around the temple. I could feel such love emanating from her heart to ours. It was breathtaking and magical and a memory I will always treasure. The music man, Jethro, her husband and guiding light played the rhythm and sang to complement the magic of her voice and we were transported to a different feeling of bliss that only music reveals to those who can hear. We all enjoyed the first song immensely. I gently touched my arm to make sure I was awake and not in a dream vision experience. I had to admit that I really wouldn't have cared either way!

Prem and Jethro began talking and sharing stories with us. We were all transfixed. They said how happy they were to be performing for us and began to sing another song. Two more of my favourite songs were played and then Prem and Jethro encouraged us to sing along with them to the chorus of Claire's Song. Having overcome my fear of public singing at the retreat with Dr John, I began to sing the chorus lyrics. Others joined in quietly. As we kept singing I looked across at Prem who encouraged me to sing with her as we shared the love of music. It was a joyous, exciting experience.

As I watched Prem and Jethro performing I felt the beauty of the love that transpired between them. In my heart, I believe they are the Divine Union Relationship. It was an honour to share time and music with them. As they played their beautiful music they connected together as if they were one complete whole person, not two. I know this is a difficult concept to comprehend. But, it's true. The sacredness of love was alive and being shown to us. Their love and compassion was a real living energy.

The ambient feeling that filled us was sustaining and none of us wanted to interrupt the beautiful experience we had been a part of. But, eventually, the evening came to an end. We said goodnight and Lilly and I walked to the car. I was on cloud ninety-nine. Tomorrow was the last day of the workshop retreat and I went to bed with the melodic sound of Sacred Earth playing their tunes of love in my ears.

The next day dawned and sunshine peeked through the white

silk curtains in our room. It was a beautiful day in Byron Bay and we were excited to begin the final day of the retreat. Lilly and I felt revived and energised beyond what we would have expected. The retreat had been wonderful and we had enjoyed it immensely.

We arrived at the temple and found our seats as the morning session was ready to commence. Blake continued to share his wisdom teachings. More people spent the morning session shedding tears, ready to begin the release of painful life situations. They had decided to let go and heal and had accepted that help was available for them if they chose that path. It was life-changing for many of the students. The morning passed quickly.

After morning tea Blake asked us to meet in the meeting room for the daily Chi Gong session. I walked confidently into the room ready to participate. The realignment I had experienced during the Chi Gong session was now something I cherished. My muscles were becoming used to the movement and I found that I could follow his lead effortlessly. At the end of the session, Blake explained that he was going to lead us into a meditation.

We were all encouraged to lie on the floor and quieten our minds. Quietening the mind isn't easy to do. I took a few deep, slow steady breaths and found the centre in my heart. I was becoming accustomed to the fact that Blake had a unique way of encouraging healing. He then explained that he was going to take us into a deep meditation that would assist us to release any pain or suffering we had stored there.

I lay on the floor. Nothing happened for quite a while. Or, so it seemed. Without warning I felt an overwhelming, almost morbid fear of someone trying to take my life. And what was worse, the people trying to take my life were my family who were supposed to care for me, to take care of me and make sure I was safe.

Without knowing why, I had often questioned why I felt inadequate, extremely shy and uncomfortable in my own skin. A few years prior to the retreat during a trip to Adelaide – I was thirty-three at the time – I had been told a family secret.

I remember when I was told this information that I understood completely how difficult the situation must have been for my mother and father and for my grandparents. The times and the culture in the mid-sixties were restrictive and very different to the time in which we live now. It was then explained to me that my grandmother organised for a female nurse to give my mother an abortion. Fortunately for me, my father came to visit my mother and stopped the abortion from taking place. The nurse had used a knitting needle in her attempt to take my life.

As I lay on the floor in the meeting room, I released pain and fear and I cried for a very long time. I was drenched in tears. And as I lay there I could only imagine how terrified my mother must have been. She didn't understand what the adults around her were doing. My mother was born deaf and mute, and communication was restricted, so she would have been terrified. And so, I cried for her, I cried for my mother. My grandmother was trying to protect her daughter as she didn't believe my mother would be able to take care of a baby by herself. And so, I cried for her, I cried for my grandmother. The nurse was trying to help an unwed mother, a disabled girl who needed care herself. And so, I cried for her, I cried for the nurse. A tiny foetus, a brave little girl who was developing inside her mother's womb, a place where she should have felt loved and protected, was terrified and alone, knowing that death was imminent. And so, I cried for her, I cried for me. And it felt like my heart, body, soul and mind had been cleansed. This unknown pain I had been carrying deep inside my subconscious awareness was now set free.

Blake quietly urged us to sit up and become aware of our surroundings. My eyes, still red from crying so much hurt from the glare of the sun. I put on my sunglasses, partly to protect my eyes, but mostly so that other people wouldn't ask me any questions. I wasn't ready to share my experience. It was very raw and personal to me. It was time for lunch and I was so happy to be able to sit for a while and be alone.

Lilly came over to where I was sitting and asked me if I was alright. I explained that I had just experienced a massive release. She suggested I go outside and sit near the willow tree and said she would bring me some lunch. I gratefully agreed. Within ten minutes Lilly was sitting beside me with a plate of beautiful food. We ate in silence for some time and then I told Lilly what had occurred in the meditation. It was clear that I was still overcome by the enormity of what I had experienced so Lilly left me on my own to process what had transpired.

I lay on the grass and watched the birds hopping along on the grass, hoping someone would leave food for them to eat. They were friendly, chirping a happy song as they went about what they were doing. And I felt comforted. It was as if they knew that I needed loving attention. Slowly, I began the early stages of processing the release of a limiting pattern and a painful memory I had stored within me.

I was aware that I had worked on my feelings of abandonment. But this memory wasn't abandonment, it was a morbid fear of someone trying to take my life. And I remembered what it felt like to not belong, to know that my existence wasn't secure in the world. I really didn't feel that I belonged to anyone or anything. I now understood why I hadn't bonded with my family in my early childhood. Trust hadn't been formed in the very beginning. Yes, now I understood and was ready to release this limiting pattern and fear and replace it with acceptance, love and belonging.

It would have been an easy option to leave the workshop retreat after lunch and not finish the afternoon session. For a few minutes, I contemplated doing that and then I decided it was important to finish what I had started. So, with a heavy sigh I picked myself up off the grass and ventured inside the temple. The final session was ready to begin!

As we sat together as a group to complete the last session, Lilly sat beside me and offered me two slices of dark mint chocolate. She could read my mind.

With a grin, she said, "Chocolate soothes everything."

"Well, some things at least," I replied. Dark mint chocolate and peppermint tea. A combination made in heaven.

Blake asked us to retrieve our work books and begin the exercises. Suddenly, he stopped what he was doing and declared, "Before we do that I would like to talk about the meditation session we had before lunch."

Momentarily, I froze. I didn't want to discuss the meditation or the experience I'd had. But perhaps I needed to talk about it more than I realised. Other people began sharing their experiences. Some were light and carefree; others were deep and meaningful.

Then Blake looked at me and said, "Tala, is there anything you would like to share?"

It was decision time. Tears started rolling down my cheeks. There was a hushed silence in the room. I managed to say that I had faced a painful life experience in the meditation. Blake, wisdom teacher and guide, encouraged me to share what had transpired.

I knew that if I shared my experience it would help me and also be the catalyst for change and growth in others. So, I took a deep breath and shared with the group what had happened to me as a baby. The group gasped in unison and many shed tears of sorrow and sympathy.

What transpired next was an open discussion that changed the dynamic of this group. Each person was able to go to a deeper place of pain to share and release a deeper emotional pain than ever before. It was cathartic. I found that I could cry and express my pain and fear while in this safe environment. Even though I could find empathy for my family members, it was fear that kept me stuck. I was afraid to be successful. What if I achieved all my dreams and goals? Who would be there to support and encourage me? Fear of failure felt like an old friend. It was a limiting pattern I had healed many years ago. Fear of success was a different matter entirely. What if I let fear block my success in teaching the Divine Union Relationship? If my family didn't want me to be here on the earth, who could I lean on for love and support?

Illusions that created fear patterns kept circling in my head like a merry-go-round. In truth, they weren't real and it was time to acknowledge that and let them go. With the help of others, I could and would achieve my goals and dreams. Success was mine if I wanted it. Blake looked at me and smiled. He knew that I had shifted a dramatic limiting belief during the workshop and that was the reason I had attended. My life would now move forward in a really positive way.

The workshop retreat had come to an end. We said fond farewells and, after thanking Blake and his team, Lilly and I said goodbye. It was time to begin the next stage of our journey. Unbeknown to me, in a very short space of time, I was going to meet the fourth aspect of love.

Chapter 22

The Three of Us

The workshop retreat concluded and Lilly and I headed back to our accommodation. After an early night, we spent the next few days looking around the Byron Bay Shire and relaxing at the beach. We wandered into boutique shops and found beautiful jewellery and art work. A little retail therapy uplifted us. On the spur of the moment, I bought a few new outfits that would be perfect to wear to the summer breakfast events.

The next morning Lilly and I decided to extend our holiday for a week as I was not yet ready to return home and we wanted to visit the Crystal Castle and Shamballa Gardens. A few things I looked forward to doing there were enjoying walks in the exquisite natural surrounds, attending some of the daily workshops and viewing crystals from all over the world. The gardens were reputed to have the largest stone Buddha in Australia and the only Kalachakra world peace Stupa in the Southern Hemisphere. This Stupa was the seventh one built of only seven in the world. There were also books, CDs and beautiful jewellery on sale. And finally, the Lotus Café was known to serve delicious food.

Lilly and I studied the online workshop program and selected some workshops we wanted to attend. I was particularly interested in a crystal bowl meditation group and there was also a mindfulness meditation class and a goal setting orientation class that I thought would be beneficial. Lilly made her own choices. As soon as we tidied our accommodation, we set out for a day of learning and adventure.

The drive to the Crystal Castle took twenty minutes and within a few minutes we had put the coast behind us and the winding road ventured toward the rainforest up into the hinterland. The views were breathtaking but the roads were a little steep. I decided not to look down the deep gullies. It was a very long way down. I just kept thinking positive thoughts. Lilly and I listened to my new Sacred Earth CD and memories of my magical night singing with them resurfaced. The beautiful memories, that I treasure still, made me smile.

Finally, we arrived and parked the car underneath trees with long hanging branches that provided some shade. It was humid, sticky and really hot. I love the heat so I was quite happy in that regard. Humidity, however, is another matter entirely! It was constant and unrelenting.

The walk to the entry took a few minutes and we paid the entry fee and were given a beautiful brochure to peruse which included a leaflet detailing the classes and workshops. Our first classes were ready to commence so Lilly and I organised to meet in the café at 1.00 pm for lunch.

The Shamballa Gardens were stunning. Tall trees stood strong and majestic. The crystals scattered around the grounds were breathtaking. I walked along a curved path and found the meditation room. There were people sitting on yoga mats, quietly preparing for meditation. I adore the sound of crystal bowls. The reverberation is in complete harmony with the Divine Union and quality of sound takes me to a special inner sanctum. I found a spot in the middle of the room and sat patiently, waiting to begin.

After I sat down, I looked around the room. Twenty people had gathered together to meditate and listen to the majestic sound of the crystal bowls. A noise drew my attention toward the door and a man entered, found a yoga mat and sat beside me. He was approximately six-foot tall, solid build with golden-honey coloured hair. His aftershave smelled like cinnamon with a hint of vanilla. I took a small breath, inhaled and sat with the aroma. My inner being reacted immediately. Wow, there's that feeling again. The feeling that, somehow, I knew this man and that he was here for a reason.

The meditation teacher entered the room and began to share information regarding the crystal bowls. She asked if anyone had heard about them before. I raised my hand and the handsome man beside me did the same. He turned his head and looked at me. I mean, he stared deep into my soul. I smiled at him. That took me by surprise. I'm usually very guarded when people want to look deeply into my eyes. Usually, I back away when someone tries to do that. I'm not sure why but I knew that I was safe with this man and that he was looking for a kindred spirit. His eyes were the hue of rich brown honey. They sparkled when he smiled. There was something special about this man. Very special indeed! He emitted an emotionally calm interior and exterior.

The teacher instructed us to lie on our yoga mats in preparation for the meditation. She was using seven crystal bowls for the meditation exercise. Each bowl correlated to a particular chakra. The seven chakras are: base chakra, sacral chakra, solar plexus chakra, heart chakra, throat chakra, third eye chakra and crown chakra. As I lay on the floor I was aware of the man's presence. It was delightful. Before my mind could tell me more information, the harmonic convergence of the bowls hit my heart with full force. The heart chakra bowl was being played.

For a moment, I felt like I was being twirled and whirled on a merry-go-round ride. My head felt dizzy and I wanted it to stop. Within a few minutes, the dizzy feeling passed and my body responded to the different sounds. Five minutes later I was feeling blissful and free.

Without warning, the stranger beside me had released his soul and it was beginning to connect with mine. Losing the constraints of the physical body was exhilarating. It created a freedom and purity that was similar to my past experiences. He moved his arm around my waist and pulled me close to his body. His lips were touching mine and I felt the sacredness of a kiss. Yes, a deep kiss, the kind that curls your toes. Ah, the bliss!

My body started to vibrate in the way I had become accustomed to. I felt deeply connected to this man and I knew that we were having an energy experience. However, for the moment we were strangers so I pulled my soul's energy back and refused to continue to participate. Reality prevailed. I could sense his confusion and disappointment as he withdrew his energy. My past experiences had prepared me for what had just transpired but I needed more information before proceeding further. His first name would be a good start!

The meditation lasted for another twenty minutes. My chakras had been cleansed and as I came back to my inner heart centre I felt lighter in my emotions, mind and body. The teacher urged us to move slowly and sit up when we were ready. As I stretched my legs I wondered how the man beside me was faring? Did I want to look into his eyes to see if he recognised what had transpired between us? No, not really. I was hoping that he didn't remember or know anything at all.

Within a few minutes everyone was sitting up. No one was talking, we were all enjoying the bliss of our meditation experience. The teacher asked if anyone had an experience they would like to share. A few ladies shared their experience of feeling bliss, some said they felt lighter and some said that they drifted away to a favourite place or sacred space they had visited often. I still hadn't looked at the man sitting beside me deciding that avoidance was the best course of action!

The meditation session was being drawn to a close when the man beside me asked if he could share his experience. What was he going to say? I wondered. The teacher nodded her head and said yes. I held my breath as he began to speak to the group.

"From the beginning I felt as if I was floating on a cloud," he stated. The group were listening intently to his words. "Then I felt my soul leave my body," he said in a calm, quiet voice. By this stage my cheeks were blushing rosy pink. I took a big sip of my water and covered my face with my hands as if listening intently. I couldn't look at him. Instead, I looked at the teacher as she waited for him to continue speaking. She was watching him with keen interest.

He continued, "Once my soul was free I felt liberated and light. The next moment I was beside a beautiful woman. Her soul was the colour of spun gold with white flecks of shimmering light. No woman I had ever seen or known before has possessed this kind of beauty. I can't explain why, but I knew her and I was drawn to her like a magnet. I just couldn't help myself and I put my arms around her waist and drew her to me. She didn't resist. I knew she too felt the connection. I felt her pull toward me and she willingly stepped into my arms." As he stopped to take a breath, everyone's eyes were riveted on him.

"Before I knew what was happening I was kissing her," he said. "It was a deep soulful kiss that shook me to my core. I am a man and I've kissed women before but never like this. I don't know what just happened to me. Abruptly, the kiss ended and I felt a sense of loss I can't explain. As if I had lost something sacred and precious."

You could have heard a pin drop in that room. No one spoke, no one said anything at all. We were all transfixed by this man sharing his experience. The teacher dropped out of the reverie we were all caught in and asked him to speak to her at the end of the session. She said that it was an amazing, magical experience and she thanked him for sharing it with us.

The meditation session ended and I sat for a while, looking at the floor. The man beside me said nothing and walked toward the teacher to talk to her. I rolled up my yoga mat and headed toward the door, wanting to escape as quickly as possible. "Well, that answered that question," I said to myself. He was definitely aware of what we had experienced. But thank goodness he didn't know it was me. Now it was time to meet Lilly for lunch and share my meditation experience.

Lilly and I met at the café and selected our lunch, ate quickly and then took a walk around the beautiful gardens. After a while, we found a quiet, shaded spot and stopped to have a drink of water. The heat and humidity had not abated, so it was important to keep hydrated.

We chatted for some time and I told Lilly about my experience with the man sitting next to me in the meditation class.

"Well it sounds like something important to me," Lilly stated matter-of-fact. "Tala don't run away from this experience or this man. It could lead to something special or he could be another aspect for you to learn from. You know how important it is to learn about the aspects for your work and that they are necessary in finding the path to your own Divine Union Relationship."

As usual, Lilly was right. I knew that I needed to follow where this path was leading me and I was intrigued to know whether I would see the man again. And I didn't have to wait too long to find out!

By 2.00 pm Lilly and I were walking to our afternoon class, a class that included exercises that would help us to connect more deeply with the Divine Feminine. My thoughts were still processing what had transpired in the morning class as I stretched out my yoga mat. Forty people were attending this class so it was being held in a larger room. The fragrant perfume of exotic flowers was wafting through the door and I closed my eyes momentarily to take it all in. While my eyes were closed, a tall man of solid build with honey-brown hair had walked in the door. Unbeknown to me he made his way across the room and sat down next to me.

The sound of the teacher's voice broke the silence and I opened my eyes. Out of my peripheral vision I could see the silhouette of a man. No, it couldn't be. Could it? The same feeling started to swirl within me. It was the feeling that I knew this man very well, I just couldn't remember how I knew him. His eyes were boring into my face, wanting me, urging me to make eye contact. There was no point ignoring him and I did want to know if he knew it was me so I turned to look into his eyes. His eyes met mine in a dance of joy and he smiled from a place deep inside himself. Then he grinned, a very cheeky grin. He knew. He definitely knew it was me! Now what should I do?

It was important to take a deep breath and stay calm. This class was going to last for two hours so we would be sitting together for quite a long time. Was he my Divine Union Relationship? It certainly felt like it, but at this stage I wasn't sure. Hopefully, I would be able to talk to him and discover more information.

When two people meet in the journey of the Divine Union Relationship, the connection happens first from within. It happens at the level of the soul. The soul is the real inner you. The connection doesn't happen in the body initially. Body attraction in the beginning is the basis for all conventional relationships. At the conventional level, physical sex will be basic. It will be pleasurable, but the pleasure is fleeting and lasts only while sex is taking place. To feel that same pleasurable feeling you need to engage in sex again.

In our youth, we have high energy reserves. Basic sex is pleasurable but it can also become addictive. The drive to procreate is strong at this stage; this is how nature intended it to be to secure the next generation so that humanity survives. Age, health and monotony can influence what happens to our human sex drive as we age. People can become hurt, frustrated and annoyed if their desires and needs are not met. The other consideration is that after conventional sex, our energy resources are usually quite depleted. We need to regain stamina and regroup. It takes an enormous amount of energy to re-energise the body.

The Divine Union Relationship, including the aspects, initially connect at the level of the soul. The soul has a never-ending supply of energy so it never becomes depleted. Also, the soul never ages. In my experiences with the Divine Union aspects, it always felt like we were touching for the first time, every time, so boredom and monotony doesn't exist in this instance. The soul is ageless; it cannot die so it doesn't experience old age. When souls see each other for the first time, it is with instant recognition or knowing and it is without prejudice or harm. Sex at this level is called divine love's expression and it is sacred, eternal and everlasting. Bliss at this level can last for days at a time. Having experienced both, I can share with you in complete honesty that expressing divine love's sexuality is far beyond the conventional sex-based relationships that some people choose to live in! And now that I have experienced soul love, I won't accept anything less.

As the class progressed, the exercises we were being taught were helpful and informative. I had been taught similar lessons in other classes but it was important to keep learning and perfecting the wisdom I had acquired. The sense of a presence beside me was strong. I tried to pretend he wasn't there and that I was sitting on my own. No, that didn't work, but it was fine pretending for a while.

The class ended and it was time to leave. As I rolled up my yoga mat, the man beside me said, "Hi, my name is Rob. I have some questions to ask you, would you mind meeting me for a chat?"

I thought for a second and then answered, "Of course, do you have some free time now?"

He replied that he did.

As we walked out of the room, the crystal bowl meditation teacher passed us on her way to her next class. She looked at us both and beamed a beautiful smile. She also nodded her head in acknowledgment, as if seeing us together was the most natural thing.

Rob and I decided to have a drink at the café and made our way to a table in the corner. The setting overlooked the magnificent gardens. It really was a magical place to be talking about the magic of the divine connection. We both chose peppermint tea and while we were waiting for the waitress to deliver our drinks, Rob began to talk.

"Thank you for agreeing to meet me," he said with a slight Scottish accent.

"My name is Tala," I said.

"It's lovely to meet you Tala and can I say that Tala is a really beautiful name." He beamed a smile so dazzling that it could have melted the butter on the table. What did we have here? Charming and attentive. My femininity was floating on cloud nine!

Rob and I sat down and settled in for a very long chat. He told me his life story in the comfortable way that some people share information with a stranger. He told me he was 50 years old and lived in Sydney. He owned a successful company in the building industry and he owned land and developed new properties. Unfortunately, he and his wife of twenty-five years had divorced three years ago but they shared custody of two beautiful children, a son and a daughter, who both were attending college in Melbourne, so child-rearing was now finished for them.

As I listened to this lovely man share his personal story with me, I felt a deep sense of loss within him. Something had happened to this man and it had upset him greatly. As Rob and I chatted further, it started to feel like we were old friends who hadn't seen each for a while. Occasionally, he would give me a grin and then flirt, just a little, to keep my attention. That was an old pattern that he needed to shift. He already had my attention and my heart was open and ready to listen to what he had to say.

Rob then asked me if I felt comfortable sharing my story with him. I explained to Rob that I was a Relationship Consultant. Because I didn't know him well, I shared a few details but glossed over the depth of problems in my past marriage. Sharing that level of detail would require trust. Once I had given him an overview of my story, Rob asked if he could share something of a personal nature with me. I agreed. Talking through a problem can be cathartic.

As I poured more peppermint tea into our cups, Rob sat back in his chair and explained that during his marriage, his wife had suffered greatly during menopause and experienced severe problems. In addition, her libido diminished and she no longer wanted to make love with Rob. At this point Rob looked a little sheepish, unsure if he should continue. I could see that he was having difficulty understanding what had happened so I encouraged him to continue his story. "I don't understand Tala, my ex-wife shut herself away from me and wouldn't let me touch her anymore. I lost my wife a long time before we divorced." The impact of his words seemed to cut him like a knife and I knew that he still hadn't resolved his feelings about this private issue. "Did she stop loving me?" he queried. "Or didn't she find me attractive as a man anymore? Perhaps she didn't enjoy intimacy with me? Tala did I do something wrong?"

As I sat with Rob, the enormity of his questions hit me like a thunderbolt. This man was suffering deeply and had many unanswered questions. I asked Rob if he had tried talking to his ex-wife about how he felt. He said he had broached the subject with her many times and that her reply was always the same. She told him it was the effects of menopause and that he just had to get used to it and accept that making love was something they didn't do anymore. "Just like that, our love life ended and my wife accepted it."

Rob explained that during the next three years he did the best he could and tried to help his wife rekindle her desire for him. "I tried everything I could possibly think of to be close to her. I was so patient for so long Tala and gave her as much space and time as she needed. And I never placed demands on her. But the more I tried to be close, the more she pushed me away," said Rob. "It was as if my touch hurt her. Sometimes, I would think she saw me as the enemy, as if I were a massive annoyance. Alternatively, she wanted me to be her protector and support her desire for financial abundance. It was so difficult for me to understand that the woman I loved no longer wanted to share intimacy with me."

Sadly, by the end of the third year, Rob said that he couldn't cope anymore and that he had an affair with a woman he met at work. "I knew it was the end of my marriage with my wife, that I had broken the trust between us," he admitted. "The frustration and hurt I was feeling pushed me into becoming the kind of man I never wanted to be."

The disarray and problems Rob and his wife endured caused their marriage to collapse. It had taken a massive toll on Rob's family life. His wife discovered his infidelity and within six months they were separated and living apart. With a deep sigh, Rob explained that at the time he felt abandoned and alone and scared. When I questioned him about his childhood he said that his mother died when he was thirteen years old. Tears gently began falling down his cheeks and he took a sip of peppermint tea and looked out the window and down into the gully below. Rob admitted he was surprised that he felt so comfortable telling a stranger his life story, and that he felt really comfortable talking to me.

We talked for another half an hour and then realised it was getting late. It was nearly closing time at the Crystal Castle. "Where did the time go Tala?" he asked. We parted company and Rob asked if I was returning during the week to attend more classes. I replied that I was. "I would like to see you again Tala. I feel very connected to you in such a short space of time. I also have a feeling that we have met for an important reason." I agreed and we said goodbye. As I walked to the car, my feet didn't seem to touch the ground. I needed to find out more information about Rob. Something was definitely happening between us!

I arrived at the Crystal Castle early the next morning. Lilly and I had agreed that Rob was definitely a man of interest and that I should see if the connection between us could deepen. Rob was sitting in the café when I walked in the next morning and he approached me as I ordered a peppermint tea to take away.

Our eyes met momentarily and I felt the butterflies in my tummy swirling. To my dismay I found myself blushing. Seriously? I tried to busy myself by looking at the lunch menu to avert attention from the pink rosy blush on my cheeks but I could sense Rob smiling. And I sensed he liked what he saw.

We headed into the meditation room and began the crystal bowl meditation class. Once again Rob was sitting beside me. The meditation teacher smiled when she saw us sitting together again. If I am completely honest, I think what amazed me was that I could feel this man's soul, his essence as soon as he was relaxed. His soul reached out to connect with me every time we met. This made perfect sense to me but wouldn't have made sense to most people. My previous experiences had proven to me that the soul does exist, that it is real.

The meditation began. The heavenly sound of the crystal bowls opened my heart and transported me to an inner place of calm, joy and serene happiness. I could feel myself floating as if buoyant in a deep pool of water and I could no longer hear or see anyone around me. The familiar sense of falling asleep overwhelmed my senses and I allowed myself to flow into the experience. A veil of sheer white curtain came into view and I gravitated towards it. With my right hand, I pulled the curtain back and looked behind the veil of the unknown. To my amazement there was a round-shaped bed adorned with a blue satin covering. I found myself moving toward the bed with a magnetism I cannot deny.

Within a few moments I saw a man appear. His body was ethereal and yet solid in appearance. Without being told I intuitively knew that it was Rob. My conscious awareness knew that he was physically sitting next to me in the meditation room. His soul, however, was there with me in the inner place, the inner sanctum where souls meet. Our souls looked exactly the same, a mirror image. The picture I could see forming in my mind was startling. Pockets of time ticked away in the physical world. Yet there, in that inner place, there was no sense of time, just the precious energy of the ever-present now. Rob was now standing in front of me, unsure of how to proceed, what to say or what to do. I smiled at him. It seemed the most natural thing to do. He returned my smile and placed his hands around my waist. Looking deeply into my eyes he searched my face for a glimmer, for a flicker of approval that I would allow him to touch me.

Our eyes locked in a dance known only to lovers and in that moment of no time, the pulse of energy began to circulate between us. There was no time to think or feel or connect to our physical earthly senses. Our souls were leading the way forward and we were the willing participants. With grace and infinite gentleness, Rob bent down and placed his lips on mine. It was a kiss that held the beauty of reverence and the exploration of pioneering new concepts contained in the Divine Union Relationship. His kiss was gentle and sweet, yet filled with so much passion that it took my breath away. In this experience, I felt the purity and beauty contained in his soul. Within a few minutes it changed and morphed into electric energy. There was an urgency to discover more. This wasn't just a kiss. It was so much more than that. This experience conveyed the truth and beauty that is contained in the soul. It was soulful, pure and exhilarating.

The kiss ended after a few minutes. Rob raised his eyebrow in a cheeky and inviting way and indicated toward the bed. It looked very inviting. To explore energy and passion with him would be wonderful. A part of my soul was ready and waiting to participate. The other part of my soul was unsure about how to proceed or what to do next. Deep within my heart I knew that something was not quite right. I shook my head to decline his invitation and, in that moment, I heard the teacher reminding us that it was time to return from our meditation. Saved by the bell. Yes, saved by the crystal bell!

When we returned from our crystal bowl meditation, I felt a myriad of emotions. I was elated and yet a part of me was disappointed that I couldn't explore a deeper soul connection with Rob. Something was blocking us from continuing the soul exploration. I turned my head and looked into his eyes, sensing his disappointment and frustration. Rob quietly leaned over and asked if we could have a chat later. I agreed and we organised to meet at the café later that afternoon. The meditation session ended and we headed outside to enjoy the fresh air.

I spent the afternoon walking around the Shamballa Gardens, looking at the large crystals and feeling more peaceful than I had in many months. The grounds were beautiful. They emitted their own kind of magic. I pulled my journal out of my bag and began writing pages of notes about my experiences during the past few days. There was much to think about and it would help to formulate my thoughts when I spoke to Rob later in the afternoon. The next three hours passed quickly and it was time to meet Rob at the café.

After ordering two pots of peppermint tea, I found a table outside the cafe in the sunshine. Rob walked in the door and waved when he saw me. He sat down next to me and we enjoyed a few minutes of general chatting before he brought up what was on his mind. "Tala, I could feel the same feeling in today's meditation that I did yesterday," he said. He told me exactly, word for word what I had also seen and experienced. We sat deep in thought for a while, sipping our tea before speaking again.

"What do you think it all means," Rob asked.

"I'm not too sure," I replied. "Our souls want to experience this profound connection between us."

Rob asked why I had hesitated to allow our experience to go further. The pull toward him was really strong and I had wanted to go further with our experience. I couldn't define it, but something had stopped me. It took all my strength to remain calm and focused. Rob knew that I was holding back, that something inside me was yelling no! We chatted for another half an hour and then said goodbye. There was one more day to go.

The following morning, I arrived at the meditation room and found to my surprise that Rob wasn't there. I remember thinking it was odd and then put the thought out of my mind and concentrated on the morning's class. That morning we were discussing our life purpose and future direction and it was heart-warming to talk to other people about my work and many of the women present took my card to book appointments to see me at a later date. The session ended and I left the room to meet Lilly.

As I walked around near the water fountain, I saw Rob standing talking to a group of people. A flicker of remembrance filtered through my mind and I remembered that Rob and I had already met. He had booked a Divine Union Relationship consultation at the festival in Melbourne earlier in the year. The memory returned in full force. He was facing a major life event, a cross-road and he needed to choose the path to love. At the time, I hadn't realised that I would be part of this man's destiny.

Rob saw me out of the corner of his eye and turned to wave to me and indicated that I should join them. With a foreboding feeling in my stomach I walked toward the group. A very young woman stood next to Rob. She had long blonde hair and was wearing short white shorts and a see-through white lace top. Her friends were standing next to her. They were laughing and giggling like young girls do. Momentarily, I thought Rob had brought his daughter and her friends with him. With a cheery smile Rob said, "Tala, I would like you to meet my partner Kim."

Wow! I tried desperately to hide my surprise. At no time during the week had Rob mentioned he had a partner. I was so surprised that I managed a quick hello and wished them a lovely afternoon and tried to make a hasty exit. Rob grabbed my arm gently and asked me how the morning meditation was. I told him it was lovely and that the group enjoyed the session, whereas, all I wanted to do was get away from Rob and Kim as quickly as possible. Feeling really silly, I wondered why we had shared a deep connection at all.

Rob asked to talk to me for a few minutes and I agreed as I was curious to hear what he had to say. "Tala it was so lovely to meet you. I really enjoyed our experiences together and I am really keen to continue to explore what we have already shared. You are amazing and your energy and heart is so pure," he said. "I can't wait to see where our explorations will take us. Can I have your mobile number please?"

Out of my peripheral vision, I noticed Kim wasn't at all happy with Rob's interest in me. Nor should she be. Rob had crossed a line and wanted to take liberties that I wasn't prepared to allow, given that he was already sharing his life with someone else.

I took a few moments to gather my thoughts. "Rob, I'm not interested in exploring the soul of a man who already has a partner.

I wish you well in your exploration and your journey. It was lovely to meet you and I really hope that everything goes well for you in your future with Kim."

Rob looked deeply into my soul for a few minutes. He was incredulous that I didn't want to share his affection and life with another woman. But I knew within my own heart that Rob needed healing. He wasn't my Divine Union. He had put another woman's happiness before me. He also wasn't able to get to know me as a partner or to commit. He already had a partner!

Rob looked into my eyes and said, "Tala, I didn't have a choice. I couldn't go through another relationship with an older woman who would go through menopause and shut off from me sexually. So, I chose a younger woman to explore my life with. Kim has oodles of energy and is a very passionate young woman. She never denies my physical needs and we have sex twice a day. I've just built a new house in the Blue Mountains and we are going to get married and start a family next year."

"Wow," I replied. "Rob I really am happy for you. I wish you and Kim the very best of luck." I smiled and quickly turned away and walked towards the gardens.

Lilly found me wandering by the water fountain and suggested it was time to go home. It had been an amazing week but the disappointment I was feeling about Rob stung just a little! I thought initially that he was my Divine Union Relationship. I had to accept that Rob wasn't my Divine Union but had introduced another aspect for me to learn about. I was getting closer to my ultimate goal. I just needed to remind myself to keep going. My Divine Union was out there in the world, waiting to meet me. He is real and I was getting closer to meeting him!

Summary: Fourth Stage of Love – Mr Upgrade

Twin Soul – Second aspect

Mr Upgrade: Mr Upgrade is the fourth stage of love and is called the twin soul connection. This is the second aspect of love. This connection is deeply felt by both individuals. The twin aspect always holds energy toward healing one or both people. The twin soul level connects couples at the levels of:

- ❖ Heart – connected to heart feelings and romantic love
- ❖ Soul – connected to the inner self, the real you
- ❖ Mind – connected to the same thoughts, values and the way you both view the world

In the second aspect of love, we see the depth and purity of the soul that draws these two people together. The souls know what to do and they feel the bond that draws them close to each other. These two souls usually connect in the dream-state. If they are spiritually aware, the connection occurs during meditation. It is like magnetism, a pull to connect and know the other twin soul. There is an intense longing to experience and connect with the twin soul. Sometimes they finish each other's sentences or they can sense the other person's emotions. The connection is felt through the soul but the attraction isn't felt initially in the body. The initial attraction is not physical, but soulful. The soul longs to express love. When two souls are sharing intimacy, physical pleasure is often experienced as different stages of sexual bliss.

After his marriage breakdown, Rob decided what he needed from his next relationship. He believed that he had found exactly what he was looking for with Kim as she would fulfil his sexual needs and desires and he believed that this would make him happy and fulfilled as a man. But he also longed for a soul connection. What he failed to understand is that he could not experience sexual desire and soul connection with two different women. Rob wanted a sexual connection in the physical with Kim and a spiritual soul connection with me. Hence, the body connection was missing in our experience of the twin soul. The heart cannot love two people at once. In my opinion, it's not possible. Guilt arises in this instance and guilt would surface in Rob's emotions regarding the other woman he wasn't with. If you are in fear you cannot be in love.

Rob had healed the grief of the ending of his marriage. He wasn't carrying emotional baggage of unresolved issues and his energy was clear and stable. But Rob carried the pain and loss of his sexuality, his inability to express sexual love as a healthy male. He still needed sexual pleasure in the physical way of a conventional relationship. The loss he endured of sexual pleasure had become the foremost condition and requirement that he placed on his new relationship. He believed wholeheartedly that the way forward for him was to upgrade to a younger woman, to fulfil his basic sexual needs. He didn't understand that the Divine Union Relationship would provide all connections of heart, body, soul and mind for him.

Not all women in their fifties are sexually inactive. It has been documented that most women still have a healthy sex drive at this age. Of course, certain medical factors do affect how women feel, but a healthy woman at this stage of her life is still able to function in a healthy sexual way.

Rob wasn't ready to consider this fact. He reasoned that if he trusted me – an older woman – with his heart, body, soul and mind, I might turn away from him sexually. His mind was made up and he moved ahead rapidly with his plan. However, the sexual pleasure he derived from his relationship with Kim didn't allow him to connect with or know her soul. His focus remained stuck in the physical component of the conventional relationship. Of course, a lot of young women are soul conscious, but Kim wasn't. Her desire for material belongings and living her life this way outweighed her desire to get to know her soul. This isn't a judgement of Kim; it is a description of her personality and how the second aspect of the Divine Union Relationship works.

When Rob met me, he discovered a soul conscious woman. I have spent years discovering the workings of my soul through my own personal experiences and years of study. I knew from the wisdom I had obtained regarding the soul that as we discover and experience the soul, we enjoy a different and more fulfilling way of life that leads to deep states of inner peace and harmony. Our lives change in a deep, almost miraculous way.

For Rob to be happy, content and fulfilled at this stage in his life, he needed two women to complete him. In reality, his choice wasn't related to our age difference. It was defined by the connection we have to our soul. Kim would definitely provide Rob with lots of sexual experiences and energy. His soul, however, would suffer because it wasn't being included. As we become more spiritually aware, physical sexual passion becomes boring and monotonous over the course of time, especially in conventional relationships. In time, Rob would be faced with the same problem and in time, would need another upgrade. They usually do!

During the course of the next few years I was informed that Rob and Kim had ended their relationship. She refused to marry him and have children because she decided he was too old for her. She was happy to receive a large financial settlement and Rob searched for a while and found his next upgrade. To do that is his right, however, his soul will keep searching for his true soul connection. For me, it was time to move forward and open my heart to the next part of the journey toward my Divine Union.

It's important to remember that an age difference between couples isn't a problem in the Divine Union Relationship. Some of the most loving and devoted couples have age differences between them. Motive and intention is always the cornerstone for any healthy, loving relationship. If a person has an ulterior motive, if they have a motive other than to unconditionally love the person they are with, then the relationship will be doomed to fail or it will create great unhappiness. Education is the best path to take to lead us forward. This is the most productive way to make informed choices. Be open to experiencing soul connection. You have nothing to lose but everything to gain!

The Fifth Stage of Love
Heart Flame – Mr Variety

The mystery of the love divine
Is hidden in the deep sunshine
Beautiful man he looks at her
Touch ignites but it won't burn
Songs to sing and wisdom to know
They meet along the destiny road
Two hearts alight when they meet
Two souls acknowledge when they greet
His passionate stare, now he can see
The beauty of her heart to believe
That she is there and so is he
This man of pure divinity
Her heart is real, her heart is true
Her love he wants to pursue
He wants to steal a sacred kiss
He wants to capture loving bliss

Stolen kisses he wants them for sure
But is he the one she's destined for?
Is she the one he can't explain
He feels the heat like falling rain
Time stands still, the feeling of love
Cascades like waterfalls from above
Perfect colours, majestic hues
He looks at her in this view
But she is wary just the same
He has problems, so she's not game
To put her heart on the line
This man who lives in the deep sunshine
He is so handsome, yes, she sees
The thought of his touch brings her to her knees
It's more than looks she searches for
It's the connection to the soul's inner core
It's sublime and real and true and pure
If he's not hers, she will show him the door
So, for now, let the fun begin
When she's in love she loves to sing
Love songs played, it's a starry night
He takes a peek in deep delight
But he will have to work you see
In helping her believe it is he
She knows the path to love divine
She knows two hearts connect, entwine
She knows the passion of the kiss
She knows the connection of soul bliss
Can he reach the pinnacle, this man of love and light?
Does he know the way to deep delight?
Will he stand tall and proud like a man?
Or will he build illusion castles in the sand?

She will have the king you see
The ultimate Divine Union for she
Only the true one will do
Only love will follow through
Nearly good enough just won't do
Keep reading now we implore you
For passion is a fiery game
They are connected, one and the same
The flaming heart will be ablaze
Into her crystal-blue eyes he will gaze
And all her secrets she might tell
From the depth of her wisdom well
It will not be easy for him
Even though she's captivated by his grin
He must be so much more you see
He must be the divine man destined for she!

Chapter 23

Colours of Love

I returned from my holiday in Byron Bay feeling refreshed and relaxed and ready to start the new year. I returned to the Research Foundation to find Tom busy looking for new guest speakers for the year. Preparations were already underway for the International Women's Day Breakfast and an all hands-on-deck approach was required to complete the amount of work necessary for its success.

International Women's Day, held on March 8, is a global day celebrating the economic, political and social achievements of women in the past, present and future. It's a day when women are recognised for their achievements regardless of nationality, ethnicity, language, culture, economics or politics. It's an occasion to look back on past struggles and accomplishments and to look ahead at the untapped potential and opportunities that await future generations of women.

Kaz Cooke, author and woman extraordinaire had graciously accepted Tom's invitation to be the guest speaker at the International Women's Day Breakfast. January and February passed quickly and soon the last preparations were concluded and the day of the event had arrived.

The ballroom was booked to capacity with over a thousand guests attending. As we ventured into the ballroom the same feeling swirled within me as I had experienced at the previous major event. It was awe-inspiring to know that so many of our local guests donated time, money and energy in support of medical research. It was humbling. Their continued support for commemorative days like International Women's Day celebrations was amazing.

As the set-up day unfolded, we set tables, organised guest lists and decorated the ballroom. It transformed before our eyes. Balloons and sponsor's banners brought colour and vibrancy to the main stage. By 6.00 pm we had completed our tasks in readiness for the celebration to commence the next morning and it was time to go home and relax. I had a quiet dinner and an early night to prepare myself for the next morning.

The next day dawned bright, sunny and warm. It was summertime. The birds were chirping loudly as if to herald this special event. The alarm whirring in my ear reminded me that it was time to embrace the day. I rolled over and hit the snooze button and for ten minutes thought about the day ahead. It was going to be a busy morning and there was much to do. My emotions were on high alert so I jumped out of bed to get ready.

After arriving at the hotel, I walked into the ballroom to see waiters delivering jugs of juice, tea and coffee to tables. Our guests who would be arriving soon. With the assistance of volunteers, we were ready to handle the large volume of people. I made my way to front of the ballroom to greet guests and assist them to find their seats. Within ten minutes a swarm of people were heading toward their tables, talking excitedly about the morning ahead.

Tom appeared looking sophisticated in his dark blue suit. He smiled a beaming smile at me and Mary and with aplomb he announced, "Show time, are we ready to commence ladies?" We both nodded and as we walked inside the ballroom a hush came over the audience. Tom walked across the stage to the microphone to address the group and the International Women's Day celebrations began!

Once the relevant greetings had been made, Tom introduced Kaz Cooke to resounding applause from our guests. As she walked to the stage, I found myself settling back in my chair to listen. Kaz smiled at the audience as she stood next to the microphone. The first thing I noticed was her hair. It shone under the brilliance of the ballroom lights and as if on cue she started her address by thanking the hair dresser at the hotel who had made her look presentable for this auspicious day. The guests laughed and she relaxed into her talk.

Kaz mentioned she was born and raised in Melbourne. She is an author, cartoonist and broadcaster and her published books include *Up the Duff, Kidwrangling, Women's Stuff, Girl's Stuff* and *Real Gorgeous* to name a few. I felt the warmth and genuine sense of humour of this lovely lady. She has an amazing ability to talk about the important things in life in an honest and truthful way. It was if we were sharing time with a new friend, a confidante. We felt that Kaz was a woman who would be happy to listen to our secrets and offer words of wisdom if we asked her. After listening to Kaz's talk, I felt inspired to complete my first book. Yes, we all have something important to say, words of value that need to be shared and heard. Kaz said that the world needs people who have words to say and that it is important to stand strong and do so. As women who had gathered together on this special day, International Women's Day, we felt a connection with this amazing woman. Our lives were enriched by sharing time together and getting to know her better.

All too soon, Kaz finished her address and the raffle and lucky door prizes were drawn. We ended the morning on a high note, ready and willing to go out into the world and make a difference in our own unique way.

My work at the Research Foundation continued and now it was time to concentrate on the monthly breakfast functions. Tom was busy securing guest speakers for the months ahead and Mary and I worked together as a team to ensure their success.

A few months later, Lilly received an invitation from Blake Bauer to attend another retreat at Byron Bay. It was scheduled for late September and we both felt that a holiday in the sun would replenish us. Lilly had healed from the grief of losing her beloved partner Yoong eight years earlier, but she still had a niggling doubt in her mind. Was she ready to purse a new relationship? On one level, she felt she was ready to embrace change and a new life direction and yet she still felt alone and unsure of the unknown future. This is an important issue and a concern that many people face.

Lilly and I booked our airfares, accommodation and tickets for the retreat. At that time of year, Byron Bay isn't as humid as in mid-summer so we looked forward to more tolerable weather. The months passed quickly and the day before we were due to go to Byron Bay I packed my suitcase in preparation for our three-day trip. It was amazing that I now looked forward to flying and the panic attacks were a distance memory.

The next morning, I woke with a foreboding feeling inside and the beginning of a head-cold. Within half an hour my chest was congested. I called Lilly and apologised profusely, explaining that I thought it was unwise for me to travel. Lilly agreed and suggested I go back to bed and rest. Disappointment lingered during the next hour, but I snuggled under my doona with my beautiful dog, Ollie curled up next to me. I lay there feeling unwell and truly sorry for myself. I felt really disappointed.

Lilly finished packing. She had weighed up whether she should still attend the retreat or stay home. But the tickets were booked and paid for so she decided to go anyway. It was the best decision for her and there was a healing that she needed to receive. My life journey was taking me in a totally different direction to meet the next stage of love.

Over afternoon tea with friends after a meditation class, the subject of colour therapy came up. One of the women discussed her recent experience of a soul reading with an Aura Soma practitioner. Her story piqued my interest so I sought a consultation myself.

The concept of the Aura Soma equilibrium bottles was brought forth by Vicki Wall in 1983. She was sixty-six years old at the time and had become clinically blind. She lived in a small village in England. From these humble beginnings in a small English village, Aura Soma is the largest manufacturer of colour energy products in the world. The coloured bottle essences improve well-being and transform lives. The essences connect with and work directly with the soul.

The Aura Soma consultant I visited, Rebecca, was a very friendly young woman with whom I felt immediately at ease. She invited me to sit down and asked me to select four coloured bottles. My consultation revealed a deep love for others, the knowledge and wisdom to teach others new ideas and concepts and of course abilities relating to writing and creative expression. She also said that I have an open enquiring mind and that I loved learning new concepts and ideas. Rebecca gave me a very detailed analysis of my personality that was extremely helpful and insightful regarding my future purpose and life direction. I left the session feeling light-hearted and brimming with excitement about the direction my life was taking. The consultation was in alignment with my goals and dreams. I had no idea how, but I felt colour therapy would somehow be connected to my work with the Divine Union Relationship consultations in the future.

Many of my friends had consultations with Aura Soma consultants and found the guidance and life direction extremely helpful. I would often inhale the essence of a quintessence if I felt depleted in energy. Within a few minutes I could feel positive effects. I was convinced that the beautiful coloured essence held magical, healing properties. I have deep respect and gratitude for this amazing colour energy system.

A week later, I was working my way through emails that had accumulated during my convalescence and my attention was drawn to an invitation to attend an Aura Soma workshop. I opened the email and found to my delight that co-creator Mike Booth was birthing a new Aura Soma bottle number 114, Archangel Raguel. To witness this birth was an honour and a privilege.

Once I had registered to attend the workshop I felt immense heat in my heart centre. There was someone I specifically needed to meet at the Aura Soma workshop. For now, the reason wasn't evident, it was a sense of inner knowing. The workshop was scheduled to start in a few weeks. Until then I kept my mind occupied with additional study and research about the benefits of soul awareness. The weeks quickly passed by.

I arrived at the workshop earlier than I had originally planned. The need to be ready and organised came to the forefront in my mind. It also enabled me to find the perfect seat and I could relax before the morning session commenced.

The venue seated one hundred people and I found a chair next to the front entrance so that I could feel the gentle breeze that wafted through the doors. The breeze was cooling and refreshing. Group members arrived and began talking to people they knew. I placed a bottle of water near my feet and a notepad on my lap and waited for Mike Booth to arrive.

Within a few minutes I heard a voice call out my name. "Tala, how are you? It's so lovely to see you."

I looked up and saw Dan walking toward me. I was stunned for a few moments and then I suddenly remembered who he was. Dan had attended the crystal bowl meditation group in Byron Bay and when he had shared his meditation experiences with the group, he mentioned that he was looking for his life purpose path. He also shared that he had a great love of adventure and wanted to travel extensively in the future. During that time, Dan and I regularly chatted. He was friendly and polite and had a great sense of humour.

Dan said he was attending the Aura Soma workshop with a friend Jake and had promised to save him a seat. I replied that I was fine sitting where I was and that he should find a seat before they were all taken. He gave me a puzzled look and found two seats nearby.

Mike entered the workshop at 10.00 am. He walked slowly and purposefully around the room. The morning session began with an introduction to the birth of the new Aura Soma bottle Archangel Raguel. There were numerous people who wanted to ask questions about the new bottle but he said that the answers would become evident during the workshop and until then, we all needed to be patient.

The morning session passed quickly. Dan walked over to me during the morning tea break and we chatted for a few minutes. He asked if I would like to sit down as we continued to talk. The television was on and the commentator was revealing the latest Australian Cricket Test results. Without warning, Dan ran his hand down the front of my bare leg. I inhaled a large breath of air. The chemistry and connection I felt was very real. In a quiet, reverent tone he said, "Tala, I am listening to everything you have to say but I would like to hear the cricket results if you don't mind and then you will have my full, undivided attention, I promise."

Surges of energy kept running down my leg even though Dan had removed his hand. An electrical current was running between our two souls. His touch had created quite a stir. My heart was racing with excitement at the thought of his touch. His fingers had brushed along my cells and they seemed to be dancing in delight and remembrance. Dan's touch was known to me and once again, this thought filled my heart with joyful anticipation.

He listened to the cricket score and then, as promised, he gave me his undivided attention for the next half an hour. We chatted and laughed about the experiences we had shared at the meditation group. Conversation flowed easily between us and a spark of chemistry was evident. Morning tea concluded and we made our way back into the room.

Mike was ready to begin the teaching wisdom of the Aura Soma course. We started taking notes as he provided information about the new bottle. He explained that the bottle would be birthed the next evening. This course was unique as it combined knowledge and wisdom together with experiential learning. To our delight, we were able to experience the magic of the new Aura Soma bottle's essence first-hand. The smooth, silky, velvety essence played on our skin as we dabbed it on our hands. The bottle's essence has a vitality and purity that is magical to experience.

Dan made eye contact and gave me long appreciative looks during the remainder of the day. The subtle attention and encouraging looks added to the chemistry I could feel transpiring between us. It felt like a magnet was pulling us together, encouraging us to get to know one another. Even though we were surrounded by other people, it felt like we were the only two people in the room. The first day ended and we took our notes home to review them.

During the next morning session, it was difficult to concentrate. The pull to touch and connect with Dan was overwhelming and the need to talk to him was nearly impossible to ignore. The Aura Soma bottles usually captured my attention. My reaction to Dan was definitely interesting. Without warning and unconsciously, Dan brushed his leg against mine and casually touched my arm. Was he my Divine Union Relationship or another aspect for me to learn information from? More questions formulated in my mind, however, no answers were forthcoming. Dan may have important and valuable information I needed to hear concerning the aspects of love. I refocused my attention on Mike and prayed that the day passed quickly.

Early evening arrived on the 11th November. The time was 11.11 am (England time zone) The number eleven relates to portals and gateways. The timing of the birth of the Aura Soma bottle was of vital importance. The group gathered together to watch the birthing and unfolding of Aura Soma bottle 114. This bottle is connected to those who are seeking true purpose and why they are here and how to get in touch with what is asked of them. The primary focus is human relationships – the way we relate to one another. When we feel worthy inside, the less we feel a sense of lack in our relationships with others. In this way, we nurture the very core of our being. Non-intrusion and non-judgement are prevalent here. The Archangel Raguel helps us to return in harmony to our core values and principles. I now understood why I had felt drawn to attend the Aura Soma workshop. Attaining my Divine Union Relationship was my life purpose and teaching the concepts and principles was the driving force that led me toward my goals.

The birthing process of the Aura Soma bottle is a sacred process that belongs to the teaching of Aura Soma and is not mine to share. I can tell you that the process involved was highly spiritual in degrees that are impossible to describe. The room felt like we had stepped through a portal to the sacred divine. Angelic light and vibration was spectacular. It is an experience I treasure and will never forget.

The last day of the workshop arrived. My soul was preparing me for what would transpire next. As I walked toward my seat I saw Dan talking to a woman. She put her hand on his arm and slowly he bent down and gave her a sweet kiss on the lips. I sat down on my chair, unsure of what to do next.

"Oh, Tala, I would like to introduce you to my wife Catherine," Dan said.

"Good morning Dan. Catherine, it is lovely to meet you." I said then excused myself and went to pour myself a glass of water. When I returned, Catherine had left and Dan was sitting in his chair. As I sat down he looked at me and continued to talk as if nothing significant had happened.

Do unto others as you would have them do unto you.

This statement is a value system I have adhered to in my life and it has served me very well. I had my answer. Dan was married which meant that he was unavailable. He was not my Divine Union Relationship. I became less communicative with Dan during the day and I witnessed him talking to other ladies in the room. He wasn't being rude or offensive, he needed attention to fill the void in his soul. I realised that Dan was my fifth aspect of love.

The afternoon approached and Dan was sitting next to a beautiful young woman. He looked at me with an expression of confusion. It was important to stand my ground and proceed in a manner that I was comfortable with and I wasn't prepared to have an affair with a married man. It was that simple! I spent the remainder of the day talking to other people and enjoying myself immensely. The workshop had given me new information and tools I required to complete my life purpose.

The Aura Soma workshop concluded and Mike gave us our certificates of merit. I walked toward him to accept mine and he gave me a hug and smiled. He congratulated me and thanked me for sharing my wisdom with group members. I was inwardly humbled.

Dan eventually returned to his seat next to me and turned to face me. We talked for another few minutes. It felt like Dan was waiting for me to say something. I didn't. He looked at me, confused that I hadn't asked to keep in contact with him. I wished him good luck and left the workshop. I watched as four women approached Dan to ask for his mobile number and I saw the look of relief on his face. It seemed easier for him to allow women to lead the way.

As I reached my car, I heard footsteps behind me. I turned around to find Dan. "Tala", he said, "can I talk to you for a moment?"

I nodded in agreement.

Dan began by saying how much he appreciated the time and connection we had shared during the workshop. He also said that he wanted me to know that he felt a deep soul connection and attraction. "The situation I am faced with is that I have a wife that I love very much. Not everything is good between us, but I love her so I can't ask for your number as much as I would like to. She has my heart. I hope you understand that if I were a single man, I would love to get to get to know you better. I'd do that in a heartbeat."

I looked deeply into Dan's eyes and knew he was telling me the truth. The soul connection I felt with him was intense. His sincerity and honesty touched my heart and I was grateful that I didn't have to spend the next few months wondering if Dan was an aspect or something more significant. He was my Heart Flame connection. It was time to move forward to my Divine Union Relationship.

Chapter 24

New Horizons

When I returned to work, significant changes had occurred while I was on holidays. Mary had accepted another position and was leaving the Research Foundation. We were all sad to see her leave but excited that she was embarking on a new life path. Tom hired a new office manager and we welcomed Emma with open arms. She had extensive experience, was well travelled and excelled at two other languages. Emma was an asset to the foundation and Tom was thrilled to have her join the team.

As Emma settled into her new role with ease and grace, I was looking for full-time work. It was with real sadness that I explained my situation to Tom. While he understood that it was time for me to make life changes, he wasn't able to offer me a full-time position. Therefore, it was time for me to find new employment. At the same time, Lilly and I were researching our next holiday destination.

During the next twelve months, I concentrated on my work at the Research Foundation and on physically taking care of myself. I had lost weight and felt healthy for the first time in many years. My exercise regime was simple and effective; I would walk every day for thirty minutes. As each month passed my dress size decreased. Becoming the best, healthiest version of myself aligned with my role at the Research Foundation and the team I worked with supported me, giving me lots of encouragement. Their encouragement assisted me to stay on track and know that the hard work I was doing was showing positive results.

Our new office manager, Emma was a bright star with huge energy resources and a desire to succeed. She was talented and effervescent and Tom had high expectations for her. He saw her as a potential future CEO of the Research Foundation and started grooming her for this role.

One Monday morning I was called into Tom's office and asked if I would like to accept a full-time position. I was delighted as the opportunity was so unexpected. I was asked to co-ordinate the breakfast functions as well as perform my administration duties. Thrilled beyond measure, it took all of three seconds for me to say yes. I loved working at the Research Foundation and was only half-heartedly looking for a new position. The plan was that Emma would facilitate my training and simultaneously prepare for her new role. It was a decision that everyone was happy with, although, I did sense slight uncertainty from Tom. He saw my role as administration officer as limited and given my lack of training in the area of event co-ordination, he wasn't sure I was capable of handling the new role. I sensed his hesitation, however, the words remained unspoken.

Within a few months, I was given my first breakfast event to organise. I relished the opportunity to grow and expand my duties. Organising a household with four children enabled me to showcase my flair for organised precision and detail. The monthly breakfast events went smoothly and were a great success. After the event, as we sat down to enjoy breakfast, Tom congratulated me on my success in running the breakfast event smoothly and efficiently. He explained that he was very impressed with my abilities. I smiled within, being very aware of how capable I am. Running the events was effortless and natural for me, it was as if I was born to do just that.

My confidence grew and Tom relaxed more with each passing month. Our breakfast attendees commented to Tom that they were very happy with the way I organised the events. It had now become a social event for them as well. They also said that they loved the personal touches I added. As they were supporting the Research Foundation, I was supporting them and showing them in simple, yet profound ways how important they were to us. The functions were handled with care, attention and personal detail. It was growth and nurturing just at the right time.

As my confidence grew and I blossomed more each day, the biggest event was looming. The Christmas Breakfast was only a few months away and Emma was an amazing support and sounding board for me. The date was set and the invitations were designed and emailed to our guests. Our guest speaker for the Christmas Breakfast was Geraldine Doogue. She was so admired and respected as a journalist, seeker of truth and an amazing woman. I remember feeling a little overwhelmed that I was going to meet her in person.

As planned, the Christmas Breakfast set-up day arrived. It brought the community together and our attendees loved being part of something bigger than themselves. The ballroom was a blaze of colour with decorations glowing as we added the final touches. I walked around the ballroom checking that glasses were sparkling and clean, cutlery was spotless and that the table numbers were correct. The feeling always stayed with me as my feet ached and screamed for a little reprieve. Ah, to sit for just a moment would have been bliss but the job at hand needed to be completed before I could give in to the luxury of sitting down to rest. Finally, I was content that the ballroom was perfectly set and that we were ready and prepared for the next morning's celebration.

The big day arrived. One thousand guests were ushered into the ballroom. The sighs of excitement and positive comments from new guests always made me smile. Tom in his usual effervescent, reverent style warmly welcomed everyone. He had a way of making everyone feel memorable and special and he will always hold a special place in my heart. His faith and trust in me never wavered even though he wasn't sure of my capabilities during the early days. A gentle hush came over the audience and they settled, anticipating the beginning of a magical morning.

Two medical research grant recipients shared news and updates regarding medical research that had transpired during the year. Trials were being conducted and many positive results were shared in many vital areas. It was heart-warming and encouraging as we listened to the reports. It also provided encouragement for our attendees that the money they were donating was making a positive impact on medical research.

With the formalities concluded, Tom returned to the stage to announce our guest speaker, Geraldine Doogue. Geraldine stepped onto the stage to a warm, appreciative applause from everyone and I settled back in my seat and prepared to listen to her address. She steadied herself, held the lectern in both hands and looked around the crowded ballroom. With confidence and surety, she began to share her life story with us. I intently watched her poise and confidence and felt inspired that I could achieve anything I wanted to.

As Geraldine progressed with her story she hesitated for a moment, looked directly at me and stated in a strong vibrant voice, "You do not have to obtain a university degree to be successful in life. You simply don't." She beamed a dazzling smile directly at me and I nearly fell off my chair. "Did that really happen," I asked myself. "No, it couldn't be true," I reasoned. How could Geraldine Doogue possibly know that this was the constant stumbling block in my life and the reason I questioned my ability to be a leader and teacher of the Divine Union Relationship. The hair on my arms stood on end as she continued her amazing story. During the next half hour, my perspective changed and I felt as if a massive block had been cleared from my heart. It was a gift she had no idea she had bestowed on me. As I looked around the room at the guests I could see that they too were inspired and encouraged by her story and the energy of this humble inspiring woman.

As the morning was brought to a close I sat for a moment, taking in the enormity of what had just transpired for me on a personal level. For so many years, I had been content to stay hidden in the background, hiding my light, the real me, so that people would see the veneer I presented to others. Some people do that. We hide our true light and then find out that we didn't receive that promotion or special advancement, the love we deserve and the happiness and pure joy we should accept. The safe place of complacency of being second, third or fourth best is adorned like a shield we wear for protection. I knew that part of my life purpose was to encourage women to be their true authentic selves and to celebrate what that looks and feels like. As we shed our limitations, fears, insecurities and self-doubt, a life-changing transformation occurs. The beauty and energy of our true light shines forth from a dark place of the shadow-side of our hidden parts. The heart is reborn!

During the next eighteen months, I organised the monthly breakfast functions and loved every minute of it. Along the way, I met more amazing women such as cook extraordinaire Kylie Kwong. Her effervescent nature and calm manner under pressure was amazing to watch. Her smile would light up the room and her gentle nature was caring and yet she was passionate in her love of cooking. Well-known actress Kerrie Armstrong held my hands in her hands and her eyes emanated bright light from her soul to mine as we greeted each other like known friends. I remember feeling a bolt of energy rush through me. Author Fiona McIntosh encouraged me to finish writing my first manuscript and to not take the knock-backs to heart, to keep my vision pure and strong towards the life path I wanted to pursue. Prominent business leaders encouraged me to keep going, to not hold back and to keep pursuing my dreams. My life opened and I blossomed in so many positive ways until one day I realised that I could fulfil my life purpose. That was a truly auspicious day.

My inner knowing knew that working at the Research Foundation was my initiation into a future world I would inherit. I was living and working through an apprenticeship, but was unaware at this stage, that I had graduated and was ready to fulfil my life purpose path. Unbeknown to me, destiny was waiting in the wings to give me the final push I needed!

What would transpire next would shock me to the core. My life was about to change in the most dramatic way imaginable!

<u>Summary: Fifth Stage of Love – Mr Variety</u>

<u>Heart Flame – Third aspect</u>

<u>**Mr Variety**</u>: This is the heart flame third aspect of love! This man will set your heart fluttering. He offers himself to you on one level and then removes himself from your life if his feelings become too intense for him to handle. In addition, his heart may not be available as it can belong to another. Connection with the heart flame happens at the levels of:

- ❖ Soul – connected to your inner self, the real you
- ❖ Body – connected to intimate and emotional attraction
- ❖ Mind – connected to the same thoughts, values and the way you both view the world

The heart flame aspect has a way of wanting attention from all the ladies! Flirting is an art form! Yes, ALL the ladies. One simply isn't enough. He also loves to be the centre of your universe but he struggles to let you into his life. This gentleman can be ultra-charming and totally attentive. For a period of time at least! He then moves on to the next exciting lady!

With this in mind, this man plays a game of hide and seek. Emotional and mental games on any level are exhausting and pointless and are a barrier to a long-term relationship forming in a healthy productive way.

The attraction you will feel to the heart flame aspect can be exciting and filled with intense passion. You will find that this aspect will usually burn out quickly with a few interactions or you may never even date this man! He is like a whirl-wind who rushes into your life and then just as quickly he can leave you with a hundred questions. You will definitely wonder what happened. That is the usual question that is asked about this man.

This third stage of love is the quick burning flame that turns into a raging inferno of feelings that can stir up your emotions in an instant. This man will open your heart quickly and engage with you as if you have been there his whole life. The degree of intimate conversation is startling and connection on a personal level will be intense. If you pursue a sexual encounter with this man it will be intense and rewarding for a moment but it will fizzle out as he will move on to the next person. This man needs and craves a variety of women in his life.

This man will have great empathy and an amazing ability to see into your heart with a clarity and purpose that will startle, excite and then confuse you. The confusion occurs in his inability to stay stable and commit to a permanent relationship with you. Mostly, you will find that this man is already in a committed relationship of some kind. And usually, there will be something missing in his current partnership that needs to be fulfilled by someone else. Alternatively, he may be single but emotionally shutdown in the heart. It isn't possible to connect on a heart level with someone who has shut down their heart to love. The connection and feelings with him are definitely exhilarating. But they are also filled with confusion and the pain of loss when he leaves.

At times, you will question whether what you did was wrong. The simple answer is that you didn't do anything wrong. You may want to wait for him to return to this incredible, amazing connection that you shared. Unfortunately, that won't happen. And you will have endless questions that he can't answer. Many hearts have been broken and hurt by the heart flame aspect and are the inspiration for many movies made about the "love that got away".

As we now know, this isn't love. It's connection and turbulence and a roller-coaster of emotions at best. The depth of connection and the lightning fast pace it creates is startling. The problem that exists here is that the heart flame aspect can be quite alluring and seductive. Be kind to yourself if you reach this stage of love knowing that like all flames, this connection will burn out eventually. However, you will rise and become like the phoenix, morphing into a greater part of yourself as the journey takes you to your ultimate destination of true love, the Divine Union Relationship.

If you find you are attached or stuck, call a friend or loved one or a professional counsellor and seek their help. Ice-cream, a glass of wine and a night on the couch with a great funny movie will do wonders for you and will return you, even if it's kicking and screaming, back to the right path. You have survived the heart flame aspect and deserve a lot of love right now! You are braver, wiser and more amazing than you know! I promise. Your Divine Union Relationship is waiting!

The Sixth Stage of Love
Twin Flame – Mr Duality

The king stands so proud to see
His aim is to please only she
Cheeky man, and handsome too
This man who steps into her view
His kingdom he will offer then
They will quickly become friends
Debonair is his way
He has such gentle words to say
She looks at him and she will sigh
She's feeling now a little tired
He lives in paradise you see
A place of beauty and tranquillity
Is he the one she searches for?
As she walks along the sandy shore?
Is he the one to call her home?
Is he the one to claim the throne?

He heals her heart from the aspect flame
She was feeling lost just the same
His energy is pure you see
The king, this man of divinity
She has left behind her home state
And landed in paradise through the gate
More time together they will spend
He is caring but he won't offend
Like a king he sits you see
And watches that she is safe with he
Grand gestures are his nature too
She's a gem to protect, that's his view
For precious and pure she is with he
And for a while she can't believe
That he adores her in his quiet way
This man who has gentle words to say
She knows the heart of love divine
She knows the pull along the vine
She knows this man's heart is true
But is he the man destined to woo?
For now, she looks and she can see
That it's a king that she perceives
But is he her king? she must explore
As she walks along the sea's sandy shore
Happiness abounds in bliss
Her soft, sweet mouth he longs to kiss?
The crashing waves upon the sea
Call her home to be near he
She feels divine when he is near
She finds him fascinating, she has no fear
Fear of love is completely gone
She listens to her favourite songs

Her heart is ready and has emerged
To be loved, honoured and finally heard
Keep reading now the plan opens wide
This king's sword is by his side
To fight for his right to be near she
He protects her heart so she can see
She must break a former love pact to grow
To clear the path to the final road
Emotions heal the bonds in the rift
Everything old sits in the shift
This man is her rock, her grounding too
The path to divine love she will now pursue

Chapter 22

Paradise Found

Destiny can surprise us when we least expect it. A great change was going to sway my life path, a change that I simply would not see coming. During the past seven years, my life had been happy and fulfilling. What I wasn't expecting was the emotional train that was hurtling toward me at two hundred kilometres per hour. The life changes that were going to unfold would affect my life dramatically. Everything was about to change!

In early January, I walked into the Research Foundation ready to embark on another amazing year and Tom asked if he could see me. I grabbed my morning cup of tea and sat down in the chair opposite him. He looked directly into my eyes and said, "Tala, I have resigned from the Research Foundation to accept another position."

For a moment, I sat there not responding, numb and shocked. I had not contemplated that this would happen. Tom explained that it was a wonderful role for him. In his new role, he could affect great change for the community and it would be his final position before retiring. Once I found my sensibilities, I offered him my congratulations with genuine care and warmth. But on a personal level, I was really sad to see him leave.

The search for a new CEO began and the Research Foundation appointed a woman, Helen. Helen had vision and compassion and would assist the foundation to achieve new objectives. It was time for change. For everyone!

For a few months, everything moved along smoothly. However, inwardly, I knew it was time for me to leave and pursue my life's work and purpose. Helen's arrival provided the push I needed. In my heart, I knew that it was time for me to go.

My two eldest sons had grown and followed their own life journeys. In doing so they had moved to Queensland a few years earlier. They lived in a rural area that was paradise with long, golden sandy beaches and an aqua-blue ocean that stretched endlessly, as far as the eye could see. Palm trees lined the streets in perfect formation as if standing to attention and lush green foliage was plentiful and beautiful. And exotic flowers, rich gold, orange and midnight-blue were draped across dark green long-stemmed plants.

The weather was magical, with the sun shining brightly against a perfect blue sky. Birds would whistle their morning calls to slowly awaken residents from a deep slumber, reminding them a new day was beginning. Each morning, many people, of all ages, would walk along the ocean shore, often with their family and friends. Cars moved along the streets as people rushed to their early morning appointments. And for those who needed a dash of caffeine to begin their day, cafés brewed coffee and served breakfast. It was a hub of colour, activity and life experiences. It was a magical and vibrant place.

Once I was firm in my decision to leave the Research Foundation, I informed Helen of my decision and she reluctantly accepted my resignation. I would miss organising the breakfast fundraising functions and miss the fun we experienced with the attendees at the events. Yet I knew the inspiration and wisdom I had gained from our guest speakers would prove to be useful in my future endeavours.

I had decided to leave my island state and relocate to Queensland. The main reason for doing so was to connect to my Divine Union. The warmer weather would also improve the health of my bones. As a result of three car accidents, the discs in my back had slowly started to degenerate. The warmer climate in Queensland was exactly what I needed. The warm days and balmy nights would be perfect.

Packing up my family home was an enormous task that also proved to be an emotional roller-coaster ride. Friends gathered together to assist me with packing and cleaning. I down-sized to the point where I took only my personal belongings to Queensland. I donated my furniture to friends as I planned to purchase new furniture when I reached my destination. Out with the old and in with the new was my new motto.

The flight to Queensland took two and a half hours and as we left the island, the dark stormy rain-filled clouds cleared and the sky became a gorgeous deep blue. White wispy clouds danced along a seamless path and left images like fairy floss. I felt as if I could almost reach out and touch the clouds as they danced and formed new patterns.

Light refreshments and a snack was served by the cabin crew and I settled in for the duration of the flight. As I looked out the window of the plane, I could see blue sparkles, almost like precious gems playing on the water. They were dancing around and sparkling like pure-cut precious gems. It was enthralling to watch. I smiled. The outline of the coast, the sandy beach and green puffy trees created a feeling of bliss in my heart. My eyes filled with tears of joy. I was home! The feelings took my breath away!

The plane touched down with a mighty thump and screeched along the tarmac making a terrible sound. The children on board were most impressed with the pilot making so much noise. They were laughing with glee, while I was trying to steady the nerves in my stomach!

All the passengers disembarked and we made our way to the baggage collection. Within a few minutes, I saw my luggage flowing down the ramp and I grabbed it quickly before it wheeled around for a second turn. The airport doors swung open and the heat and humidity hit me with full force. I took a deep gulp of air and my bones seemed to sigh in relief. The heat was wonderful.

My son Marc arrived at the airport terminal and drove me to Kawana Island. The name sounded exotic and, with large palm trees situated inside roundabouts together with other green vibrant trees, it really was very beautiful. At last, Marc turned left and I saw a large white building with orange panels. The gate opened and we drove inside an extensive apartment block. The driveway was filled with more palm trees and exotic flowers. I thought I had stepped into a movie scene. It was gorgeous.

"It's beautiful here, it feels like I have stepped into paradise," I exclaimed.

Marc smiled at me and nodded his head in agreement. "You'll love it here Mum, the weather is beautiful in winter."

I put my case in my room and then ventured to the pool and lay my towel on the lounge-chair and took a sip of my water. The heat from the sun was beautiful. I lay down and felt myself relax. The peace and quiet was heavenly. Half an hour later a couple joined me and we chatted for a while. Then they walked across to the other side of the pool area and they too relaxed, enjoying being outside in the beautiful fresh air.

Out of the corner of my eye I saw a man approaching the pool area. He was wearing a white hat, a white and blue striped tee-shirt and blue shorts. Leisurely, he walked toward the pool and sat on a chair. All of sudden he looked up at me and smiled. It was a beautiful smile and I felt myself blushing. I remember thinking that he had a handsome face and soulful brown eyes. The interesting thing was that he looked at me as if he knew who I was.

White billowing clouds appeared and I decided it was time to go back inside and unpack the rest of my belongings and settle in. I was happy that the apartment was going to be my home for the next three months.

The next morning, I went back to the pool area. The handsome man had returned and he was sitting on a pool lounge looking intently at me. He studied my face for a moment and then looked intently into my soul. I found it refreshing. It was like I was looking into a mirror, viewing a part of myself that I really liked on a platonic level. The strange thing is that I didn't feel a romantic connection to this man. I felt connected, but no romantic feelings at all.

Remembering where I was, I introduced myself and explained that I was staying with my son until I found an apartment. I explained that I had moved to Queensland to live. His look of admiration made me feel happy. The man introduced himself and told me that his name was Paul. Paul explained he was separated from his wife and was beginning to feel joyful again, that he had healed his grief. He had a friendly personality but I kept an emotional distance during our early conversations. I'm sure he wasn't used to women keeping him at arms- length. In fact, I knew he wasn't used to that at all!

I ended the conversation and started to read my book before he could say anything else. I had no idea why I was feeling so flustered and unsure of myself. Who was this man?

During the next few weeks I began to explore the island and beyond and found interesting places to visit. The Glass House Mountains, Maleny and Montville would become three of my favourite places to visit. I loved discovering the small art galleries and quaint stores and I spent many happy hours browsing and discovering new things. Along the main street in Maleny there were three book stores for me to enjoy. It really was a heavenly experience.

By the third week, I found myself walking to the café and restaurant that were situated across the road from the apartment building. The café had an extensive mural of Venice sprawled across an entire wall. I felt inspired by the mural and spent many hours there writing my book. The owner and staff were welcoming. It became like my second home and my place of peace.

As I settled in, I found myself seeing Paul a few times every day. He loved to talk, honestly, he really loved to talk. The other tenants had developed a lovely rapport with him and spoke of him in glowing terms. Most of them had no qualms accepting his lovely manner but I was aware that this charming man didn't really appeal to me in a romantic way at all. I was totally confused. For the first time in the last twenty years, I found myself unsure with no idea what was happening. I felt like I was walking in the dark with no direction or light to lead the way forward.

When I didn't see Paul for a few days, I would settle into the rhythm of paradise life. A beautiful beach was located ten minutes away from the apartment and taking long walks along the beach or sitting on the grass watching people playing in the ocean was the most relaxing thing I had done in a long time. More and more I felt myself unwinding and relaxing!

As the fourth week of my stay approached, I decided to find out who Paul was and why he had appeared in my life. Each morning I would go to the pool and wait to see what would happen next. On cue, Paul would appear, as if by magic, grinning his amazing smile and dazzling me with his charming presence. At times, it was quite enchanting to watch this man treat me with special consideration. It really was all very interesting.

In small increments, Paul and I developed a platonic friendship. His gentle manner and charismatic way should have made me swoon. But my inner radar was telling me there was something about this man that wasn't right for me! Although Paul was a lovely man, he wasn't my Divine Union Relationship!

Paul often amazed me with his grand gestures. Due to the heat and humidity in Queensland, the fire alarm would set itself off and would scream at 4.30 am that there was a fire in the building and that we all needed to evacuate immediately.

I scrambled into my dressing gown, grabbed my keys and handbag and headed out the door. As I did, I could see people walking back to their rooms with gloomy looks on their faces yelling that it was a false alarm and that we could all go back to bed. I retraced my steps, walked back into the apartment and closed the door.

After enduring false alarms six more times in a matter of weeks I, like most tenants, was beginning to get fed up. When Paul greeted me one morning, I complained to him about the alarm system malfunctions. He said, "Tala, stay in your apartment. If there is a fire I will walk through the flames to rescue you and personally carry you to safety myself. You are safe. I would protect you with my life."

For a split second I assumed he was joking until I looked at his face. Instinctively, I then knew he meant every word he had said. He had honoured and respected me. Still, it made me feel a little overwhelmed!

The third month, I spent writing my book and enjoying the creative process contained in formulating words. Paul still found creative ways to get my attention and every conversation started with him looking at me as if I were the most beautiful woman in the world. He often commented that I wore the most beautiful clothes and that he loved talking to me as often as he could.

All too soon, the end of my stay at the apartment approached and it was time for me to look for my own apartment. I had decided that Queensland was my new home. Although I missed my family I knew that this was the right decision for me. I called Lorenzo and told him that I was coming to see him for a few weeks. It was also the right time to see my other family members before permanently settling in Queensland.

My family and friends were happy to see me and we spent happy days getting reacquainted. We had a wonderful time. Of course, time flies when we are having fun and soon it was time to return to Queensland. My family and friends were hoping that I would change my mind and return to the island. I knew that would never happen. Queensland was now my home. Instinctively, I knew my future husband, my Divine Union lived there. It was a deep knowing in my heart.

When I returned to Queensland, I called Paul. When Paul heard my voice on the phone, the same feelings of attraction, respect and honour he had shown me previously were still evident. Within a few minutes, Paul was excitedly telling me that I needed to call Phillip, the apartment manager. He told me that an apartment would become vacant in the next few weeks. He was adamant that it was all going to work out perfectly.

I agreed to meet Phillip the following day to look at the apartment. When I arrived, he was standing on a platform with a hose in his hand and he beamed when he saw me. With the agility of a man half his age, he jumped down and ran to greet me. He exclaimed, "Tala, it is lovely to meet you. Come with me and I will show you the apartment." As I looked through the apartment I knew that it would be perfect for me. The only problem was that all the rooms were situated on the opposite side of the building to my son's apartment so that would take a little getting used to.

Retrieving my personal items from storage and buying new furniture was like receiving early Christmas presents. I found it really quite magical. It was wonderful filling my new home with lovely new furniture. It was the unfolding of my new life. I signed the lease and moved in. With the help of two close friends we rallied around and cleaned everything so it was sparkling.

Within a short time, my new apartment felt like home. More days were spent walking along the beach and visiting my favourite café to write my book. This was my main focus now as time was ploughing along really fast and I knew that the book needed to be completed before the New Year.

Once I settled in, Paul and I found more time for longer chats and we were able to share information about ourselves with each other. Paul was a really lovely man, a man I felt a deep connection with. However, I didn't feel romantic or physical attraction for him. He felt more like my friend. I realised that Paul felt a romantic connection with me but it wasn't reciprocated. It was important for me to be kind and treat him with as much gratitude and respect as I possibly could. Twin Flames can also be reciprocated romantic love. In his own loving way, Paul had prepared me for my own Divine Union Relationship and was the sixth aspect of love.

Summary: Sixth Stage of Love – Mr Duality

Twin Flame –Fourth aspect

Mr Duality: The fourth and final aspect of love is the Twin Flame. This person will be your mirror image in values, thoughts and strengths. This aspect is all about connection and transforming each other's lives. There are two types of Twin Flames. The first type is where one twin will feel strong romantic love and the other will not. Whereas, with the second type, the twins share deep romantic love. Twin Flames will often have difficulties entering a relationship or if the twins are already in a relationship, there will be numerous issues to deal with. The twins will feel connected to each other's heart in the way of deep care and protection. In the Divine Union Relationship, romantic love is prevalent and originates from the spirit. At this level of the fourth aspect, one twin connects to the soul. The other twin connects to the spirit. For the twins to reach the stage of the Divine Union Relationship, teaching and healing needs to occur. The connections contained in twin flames are:

- ❖ Heart – connected to heart feelings, protection and connection
- ❖ Body – connected to intimate attraction
- ❖ Mind – connected to the same thoughts, values and the way you both view the world

The reason a Twin Flame enters your life is because you are ready for the catalyst of growth and major life changes.

The twin flame connection can heal any fear you may still be holding onto in your pain body. The pain body contains all hidden/ unresolved feelings of hurt and pain that haven't been healed or resolved. The twin flame will see the depth of your beauty and will mirror your greatest strengths. Listed below are the components of the twin flame connection:

❖ It is very common to feel excitement when you meet your twin flame for the first time

❖ There is a strong recognition of the twin flame

❖ Even though only one twin may feel romantic love, the bond the twins experience reveals a peaceful, joyous feeling between them

❖ You are both able to be your authentic selves

❖ New opportunities will appear naturally

❖ You and your twin flame feel connected to each other. There is freedom to explore and get to know each other, but you aren't bound or locked together

❖ The twin flames in a romantic loving partnership will want to learn how to establish a foundation in preparation for the Divine Union Relationship

❖ There is a deep need to protect each other

The Twin Flame aspect, exquisite in nature, is the connection of spirit required to enter the Divine Union Relationship. This aspect of love can be shared between couples for many years or a short connection that lasts a limited period of time. The difficulty is prevalent for the Twin Flame who feels romantic love as they cannot imagine that the other twin does not. It is inconceivable to them that romantic love is unrequited.

So much information has been written about the Twin Flames. It is my belief that this stage of love prepares us for the future. The time of turmoil, confusion and limitation contained in our relationships is a process of the past. Pioneering the concept of the Divine Union Relationship reveals that more knowledge and wisdom is needed to forge ahead. As we embark upon the journey into the unknown, we acknowledge that preparation to enter this realm is at hand to and the new teachings of divine love can be revealed in greater measure. Our evolution demands it and our future depends on it!

The Seventh Stage of Love
Divine Union – Mr Darcy

Look upon the deep blue sea
And there you will find me
Beautiful woman stay where you are
And looks toward the night-time stars
Foam-capped tide and white sand blends
You and I will be best friends
Lovers too, I call your name
Two hearts entwined, one and the same
As if by magic I fall into your eyes
I see the real you, there's no disguise
Abiding love is what I claim
Tender love and sweet refrain
Do not hide your heart from me
I won't be deterred, don't you see
In this depth of love sublime
I pledge to you my heart divine

Whisper now my name my love
Reach to the universe and stars above
Realise that I am you
For we are one, we are not two
Love and truth will set us free
Time contracts in the dance of eternity
Know that I will ask for your hand
To marry me, our lives expand
Love divine that precious thing
I will buy for you a beautiful ring
This ring I place upon your hand
Together enraptured we will stand
In the chapel of wedded bliss
Our love is sealed with a sacred kiss
I have always known your precious heart
In truth, we've never been apart
These words today I share with thee
The depth of love I feel in me
Through the portal we must go
To connect, for our love to grow
Often, I feel you think of me
This man you know, we can't believe
Our lives are soon set to entwine
No more yours, no more mine
Precious love and life we share
To sit together as we prepare
To spend our lives together, no longer apart
I pledge to you my loving heart

Chapter 26

Through the Looking Glass

I was woken in a dream vision experience and needed a few moments to focus my attention. The feeling of bliss hit my heart with full force. Through mist I could see a woman talking on her mobile phone. As I became more aware of my surroundings, I could see she was dressed in a pink flowing silk top and white trousers. I could hear a man's voice speaking to her and I knew it was important to listen intently to their conversation, but at that stage, I didn't know why. Perhaps I was going to be given more teachings about the Divine Union Relationship.

"Oh wow, I can't believe you're in Queensland," the man exclaimed. "We can finally see each other. There many beautiful places I would love to show you. I want to experience everything with you, to see wonder through your eyes. Please let me know when I can see you."

The woman took a deep breath. I'm so sorry, but I'm not ready. It's way too soon. I've only just arrived. Please understand, I'm just not ready yet!" The dream vision shimmered and was gone!

I woke the next morning and put the dream vision out of my mind

Six weeks later, I woke in another dream vision experience. I saw the same woman talking on the phone to the same man. She said confidently, "Oh yes, it will be lovely to see you one day. But I'm a writer and I need to finish writing my book first. I can't see you until then, but one day. It will happen."

The man's eyes portrayed sadness. He felt frustrated that he couldn't get through to her, that he couldn't reach the sanctity of her inner heart. He had no idea what to do next. He replied, "That's fine, I will call you again later and ask you out again." The vision slowly shimmered and was gone!

I woke with a start and sat up in bed. "Oh, my goodness," I shouted out loud. I recognised the woman in my dream vision. The woman was me. What was I doing?

I had no idea that I was carrying a subconscious pattern but I knew I needed to shift this pattern as soon as possible. I had been working toward the meeting of my Divine Union for more than twenty years.

I walked into the kitchen and called my friend Olya. We spoke for a considerable length of time about my dream vision experiences and we conceded that I had a subconscious pattern to shift.

As we chatted, I mentioned to Olya that I thought it was time to take a holiday and start exploring the world. She agreed and a few days later, we sat down to talk about the destination. Travelling overseas was also going to open new doors of growth and expansion for me. We planned a trip to Singapore to visit temples and relax. The seven-hour flight would be a gentle introduction for me to international flights. We had lots to do to prepare for the trip. It was time to revert to my maiden name and organise my passport. And we had to plan our itinerary. It was time to get moving!

Chapter 27

The Omega Connection

A new day dawned and the sun peaked over the horizon. As I turned over in my bed a searing pain ran down my spine. I was completely baffled how this could have happened. When I went to bed eight hours earlier I was fine. I pulled my legs toward me and swung them over the side of my bed. I steadied my feet on the floor and then walked into the lounge room to find my mobile phone. I needed to see my osteopath immediately. I was due to fly to Hobart to spend the Christmas holidays with my son Lorenzo and his fiancé Catherine. While I was there, I planned to go to the Boxing Day sales. Being incapacitated by back pain was not in the plan!

I picked up the business card from the fridge and dialled the number. A bright, cheery voice answered but when I requested an appointment with my usual osteopath John, she informed me he had left the practice and moved to Sydney.

Using google, I searched the internet for other osteopaths in my area and found a female osteopath. I called her number and her receptionist quickly informed me that she was fully booked all week. "Would you like an appointment after the holidays?" she enquired. I replied that I needed to see someone straight away and I hung up feeling defeated and exhausted. By then I was in considerable pain and panic began to settle in. Calming myself down, I searched again online.

I selected one of the search results and a man's face appeared on my computer screen. His face looked very familiar to me. I was positive we had already met. I brought up his contact information and phoned the Brisbane clinic. His receptionist told me he had one remaining appointment available that day. I booked the appointment and thanked her profusely. Then I took two Panadol and lay on the couch with my heat pack on my back until the pain medication started to take effect. Two hours later, using slow, deliberate movements I was dressed and ready to leave.

My son Marc arrived promptly to take me to my appointment. As I entered the clinic I was greeted by the receptionist who gave me the relevant forms to fill in. My mind was in a blur and an unusual feeling was swirling in the inner-sanctum of my heart. At that stage, I was in too much pain to give the sensation any consideration.

Within five minutes, a tall, distinguished looking man approached me and flashed a dazzling smile my way. He reached out his hand and our eyes connected and locked for a moment and he completely forgot that he had offered me his hand. I shook his outstretched hand only to find that he was still staring into my eyes. It was as if he were retrieving an imprinted memory he had buried long ago. Startled, I stepped back.

"Hi, I'm Drew Kensington," he said. "Please follow me." Gingerly, I waddled behind him into his office at a very slow pace. He invited me to sit down and asked for relevant medical details and any previous injuries I had sustained. Within a few minutes he had collated all the information he needed and he asked me to lie on the examination table.

A warm heat began to circle my body. Drew took a pillow and put it under my knees to relieve the pressure on my back. It felt wonderful to be relieved of pain for a moment. Soft soothing music was playing in the background. He then sat on a stool and moved until he was sitting at my left side. He placed his hands underneath my upper back and began the necessary movements to ease my pain. Within a few minutes, I took a deep breath and breathed a sigh of relief. The pain in my left side had eased considerably. Drew was a very proficient and well-trained practitioner and he displayed the utmost professional care and attention. Soon I was able to relax more. With the grace of a dancer he swivelled the stool to sit on my right-hand side, ready to commence the second half of the session.

As Drew worked on my right side, he asked questions about my condition. I answered with some details about my life. His gentle, caring manner shone through immediately. We chatted freely for five minutes. He asked me if any issues were bothering me. I admitted that there were a few issues that concerned me and I felt at ease and able to chat freely with him. Slowly, I could feel the tension in my back easing considerably.

As if by magic, a bright golden light filled the room. It took my breath away momentarily. I was floating on a white puffy cloud of emotional freedom and bliss was filling my heart. I truly believed Drew and I met for a reason. At this stage, I had no idea what the reason was. I had met all the men in the six stages of love. Yet,

Drew felt familiar to me and I trusted him implicitly, yet without knowing why. In twenty minutes the session ended and it was time for me to leave. I climbed off the bed and walked around the room and I found that my movements were more flexible and I could walk with less pain. There was still stiffness in my body but the pain had reduced considerably. I booked a follow-up appointment for the following day.

The next afternoon I arrived at the clinic and Drew welcomed me in the same caring manner. I lay down on the examination table and he explained that he was going to work on my neck muscles and his hands cupped the back of my neck. His fingers massaged and moved my neck muscles gently, yet firmly.

I cannot explain how or why but I felt deeply connected to Drew. My soul knew his soul. Unseen energy began floating around the room, my physical atoms were having their own cosmic experience. It was sublime, surreal and totally unexpected. I lay quietly on the examination table until the feelings dissipated. As soon as I felt the connection again, I shifted my attention and focused on my breathing to dissipate the energy, but it wouldn't stop. It was as if my atoms had a mind of their own! What was happening?

After a few minutes of silence, Drew asked questions about my past experiences with love and relationships. He listened intently and reverently and nodded his head, understanding the point of reference I was making. The questions he asked revealed wisdom and the crooning tone of his voice was calming and relaxing. The liberation I felt in sharing my experiences opened a deeper inner reflection in my soul.

Our half an hour session contained a shift in time and it felt like we were talking for hours instead of minutes. Conversation flowed effortlessly. A gentle lull in the conversation ensued and I felt myself shifting into a meditative state.

Without warning, I was floating in a blissful state of peace. Pulsations of loving energy slid inside the inner sanctum of my heart centre. I'm not sure how it happened, but it did. The energy was intensely stronger than the usual meditative feelings I am accustomed to. It was deeply subliminal; more intricate than anything I had experienced before. Eventually, the session ended and it was time for me to leave. Drew suggested I make a follow-up appointment the next week.

As the sessions progressed I sustained two serious falls and injured my lower back. Consequently, my sessions with him increased to weekly visits to assist the healing process of the injuries I had sustained. Unbeknown to me, a greater plan was formulating and the puzzle pieces eventually would fall into place.

As I reviewed the six stages of love I conceded that my connection with Drew was baffling. I understood that he wasn't an aspect of love and nor did I believe that he was my Divine Union Relationship. Numerous questions swirled within my mind. For a time, no answers were evident.

The treatment sessions continued. At the beginning of each session Drew would place his hands on my back to begin the treatment. To my surprise I didn't feel uncomfortable or body conscious when he touched me. To keep distracted and to keep my mind occupied, I would meditate or sing songs in my head. This distraction would initially work perfectly for about ten minutes and then the connection and energy would burst through like a bright flame. The intensity of it would take my breath away. Seriously?

A few weeks later, during a treatment, I opened my eyes and looked up at Drew. I felt that he instinctively knew that I was looking at him. He opened his eyes and our souls connected. The shock of the experience took me by surprise. It happened only for a few seconds and yet it felt like an eternity. I closed my eyes and thought that I had imagined it all. Perhaps Drew was in a deep awareness too and he was feeling a state of bliss that had nothing to do with me. Nothing at all!

During the next session Drew and I chatted about the beauty of the soul and the path of evolution. We talked joyously and freely until the usual bliss of the connection between us emerged and I slipped into a deep meditative state. Drew worked on my lower back and suddenly I was pulled back into the room. Instinct and intuition prevailed and I sensed a different energy in Drew's touch. It was a touch of friendship and familiarity and our souls were acknowledging the presence of each other.

The session concluded and I sat in the chair and slipped my shoes on. I sat up and pulled my handbag onto my shoulder when I heard a plop on the floor. To my surprise, my glasses had fallen off the table and landed at Drew's feet. "Tala, don't move," he said.

I stood perfectly still and momentarily time moved in slow motion. Drew retrieved my glasses and I opened my hand to receive them. He curled his fingers around my glasses and gently placed them in my right hand. In a few seconds, I registered that he was touching my skin. Instinctively, I placed my hand over his. My cells danced around his cells and I found it difficult to breathe. We had stepped into a sacred moment in time. He gently caressed my skin as I reluctantly opened my hand to let his go. My fingers grazed the top of his and in slow, gentle increments our hands moved apart. It was delightful and I didn't want it to end.

Poets have articulated words to describe the touch of the divine and artists have created extraordinary masterpieces to encapsulate this moment. A profound experience was happening between me and Drew. Drew was an evolved man, a divine man. He just wasn't my divine man. He possessed a pure heart and an evolved soul and I was positive that he was here to teach me something of real importance.

A week later I arrived at the clinic for my osteopathy appointment. Drew beamed a beautiful smile at me and he started the session. I lay on the examination table and meditated, entering my inner sanctuary. As Drew was working on my upper back. I felt a bolt of white light energy dart up my legs and spine and exit through the top of my head. An electrical current was tingling up and down my spine. I felt no pain or discomfort in my body. My previous experiences with energy systems indicated that a significant process was taking place.

My body was exuding an immense heat which felt intense and overpowering. The heat was circulating from the inside and then filtered outside my body. In a higher state of awareness, I reminded myself to breathe and fully relax into the experience. "What could possibly go wrong?" I asked myself. I was out of my emotional depth and trusted a process I had never experienced before. Drew was busy, working diligently to put my back into balance!

The Kundalini life-force rose from the base of my spine. It swivelled and moved effortlessly to the front of my base chakra. A deep energy released in my body. I considered asking Drew to stop the treatment but an inner knowing prompted me to wait a while longer.

The energy moved into the sacral chakra and circulated between my emotional energy centre and the seat of the soul, situated below the heart chakra. The sensation felt warm and gooey like rich, thick honey. The energy moved and filled my heart centre with pure awareness, combined with solar heat. My heart expanded and opened more fully to receive loving energy.

As I became accustomed to the feeling of love in my heart centre, the energy moved into my head centre. My mind felt a small degree of discomfort as the light vibration pierced the pineal and pituitary glands. Once this feeling subsided an all-encompassing feeling of bliss radiated within my mind. The ecstasy was unbelievable.

I was completely at ease as I played and explored in the subliminal experience I was revelling in and I was content to stay there for as long as possible. Without warning, the process continued and the light vibration pierced the top of the crown centre in my head.

A silent voice was speaking inside my head. The voice said, "I AM."

Radiant light shone around my body and my inner being felt the loving embrace of our creator. Tears began to slide down my cheeks. Overwhelming sensation created an outpouring of energy that burst from within my heart centre. The river of loving energy created a brand-new cycle and light poured back through my mind, heart, soul and finally rested in my body. I inhaled a large breath of air and lay on the table. My body lay perfectly still.

The same silent voice whispered, "You have experienced the 'Omega Connection™'." These are the ancient teachings of love known as the Divine Union Relationship. It is your life purpose to present these ancient teachings in their purest and absolute form. The Omega Connection within your cosmic energy field has been activated and you have returned home.

In the beginning was the seed-atom and it contained all that is. The spirit of One became two; masculine and feminine, to be transformed and to evolve. This occurred because souls needed to experience the earthly plane of existence as limitation and deep suffering. This was necessary to allow the seed-atom to grow to full maturity and ultimate belonging. Further teachings will be given to you as you fully merge into your Divine Union Relationship.

The room began to spin ever so slightly and I found myself floating on a deep blue ocean. It felt like I had played there for hours when I realised that I was still at the clinic lying on the examination table. The harmonious symphony of sweet violins played a melody of serenity and peace and was magic to my ears. The sound of Drew's voice brought me out of a deep reverie. This life-changing experience was profoundly incredible in every way imaginable.

Drew brought me gently back into the room and I slowly sat up. I shook my head and gently moved off the bed. As I sat on the chair I retrieved my sandals. I looked up at Drew and he smiled. His eyes sparkled like luminous stars. Drew had initiated the Omega Connection.

Wafting sheer mist covers a veil of light and momentarily blinds my eyes. As I look more deeply at the scene unfolding around me I realise that I am awake and aware in a dream vision experience. I can see the silhouette of a man in my peripheral vision.

The scene quickly changes and I can see that we are both sitting in a luxurious car. The soulful crooning sounds of music is softly playing in the background. The dark haired, handsome man is intently looking at me and he says, "Tala, tell me more about your life, I want to know everything about you."

I know for certain that I am in a car going on a date to a concert. The handsome man sitting beside me is dressed in an expensive black dinner suit and I am wearing a beautiful blue dress, my new Vera Wang sling-back shoes and carrying a Kate Spade clutch bag. Excitement and nervous energy circulate within my heart centre.

The scene changes once more and I can see myself standing in the doorway to a magnificent chapel. The haunting tones of a sacred song fill the air. The back-drop consists of vast valleys nestled in the gully below. We are in the picturesque township of Montville, Queensland. I have waited for this auspicious day for the past twenty-five years so I find myself gently pinching my arm. All of my dreams and wishes are about to come true in the next thirty minutes. It's my wedding day and I am finally going to marry my Divine Union. My long dress adorned with layers of silk rustles as I step inside the massive carved wooden doors.

My family members and special friends have gathered together this day. They stand, waiting for me to walk into the chapel of love. The sound of silence and the stillness and sacred stirrings of love create a perfect scenario in my heart. Right on cue, the wedding song signals that it is time for me to move. As I take two steps forward I look toward the front of the chapel. Holding my breath momentarily I gasp at the scene before me. Standing at the front of the altar are two men.

"What are you doing here?" I ask the man I already know. He is standing on the right-hand side of the chapel and he grins and my heart stops, but just for a moment.

He replies with a charming smile,

"Tala, you have an important decision to make. The next stage of your life path is very important. There will be two men to declare their love for you. You will have to choose which one is your Divine Union! The quest isn't over. It's only just begun!

The vision slowly shimmers and is gone.

My suitcase was standing near the door, packed and ready to take to the airport. I held my passport tightly in my hand as I made my way outside the apartment building. Today Olya and I were setting off on an adventure to Singapore. My first overseas trip. Travelling business class was an extra treat and a special bonus. It was time to experience more miracles and incredible life adventures. The map of the Divine Union is alight with new possibilities. Are you ready to explore this new adventure?

A New Heaven Upon a New Earth begins!

Summary: Seventh Stage of Love – Mr Darcy

Divine Union Relationship

Mr Darcy: The seventh stage of love is the Divine Union Relationship. It is Mr Darcy. It's the ultimate love that we can experience. The seventh stage of love is the ultimate love story. It is imperative to remember that the Divine Union consists of the connection of heart, body, soul and mind.

Mr Darcy is the final stage. In the Bridget Jones movies, we see the charming Mr Darcy try to convince Bridget that she is beautiful and perfect for him in every way. He tells her that he especially loves her jiggly parts. And he does. He loves every part of her unconditionally. There are no conditions placed upon the love that he feels and gives to her. In the beginning, she's not convinced. But by the end of the third movie, Bridget concedes that she loves him unconditionally as well. She does have it all. And of course, Mr Darcy is thrilled!

When the divine couple meet for the first time, the connection is immediate and intense. Usually, there are no obstacles in this relationship. Occasionally, if a problem does arise it will be found in a limiting pattern or belief from a previous relationship stored in the subconscious awareness. The obstacles to overcome in the final stage are self-image. It can be body issues, lack of self-esteem, not knowing who you are, hidden phobias and fears, and the stress of unrealistic pressure we can place upon ourselves to be perfect. Social media can be alarmingly brutal at times so it's important to clear away any negative issues before you meet your Divine Union Relationship.

Cleansing and clearing the chakras is the first place to start. Without knowing why, most people have difficulty letting go of past relationships. Each time you connect sexually with a partner, your chakras, which are spinning vortices of energy, merge you and your partner's energies together. Without cleansing and clearing the chakras, people stay connected to each other after the relationship has ended. When the next relationship arrives, the energy of the previous partner is still there. As you can imagine, over time, you may have past memories of previous energy partners vying for attention, wanting to be heard. The chakra balance is likened to an internal shower and is a powerful way to take back control of your life and remove your past partners once and for all.

Moving to Queensland was a major turning point in my life. I felt healthier, happier and more content living in the sunshine. All my life I had been told and been subject to messages that being thin is beautiful. Media and magazines add to the confusion and create a false sense of what beauty really is. What does it mean to be beautiful? Beauty is in the eye of the beholder. It's true. To your Divine Union you are perfect and beautiful in every way, unconditionally.

I, like Bridget wasn't prepared to show my Divine Union my jiggly parts, the curves that indicate our femininity, that make us women. I felt ashamed and upset that I wasn't young, perky or perfect. In my confusion, I believed that my Divine Union deserved the best and fervently wished that I could turn back the clock and be twenty-one again. In reality, of course, that was never going to happen. My subconscious had locked this pattern in a hidden place connected to my pain body. The pain body or shadow side is a state of awareness within ourselves where we store painful situations and experiences that have happened to us. They remain unresolved until the pattern or belief is cleared.

Rebalancing the chakra system is a safe way to bring yourself back into alignment. You deserve to feel amazing, balanced and whole and to love yourself unconditionally, all of you! It takes courage to grow and change. It takes courage to open your heart and accept that cleansing and clearing is essential to access the Divine Union Relationship. I can promise you that it will be the most incredible thing you can do!

The Divine Union Relationship is easy! Love is easy, amazing, divine and simply out of this world. Conventional unhappy relationships are painful and difficult to live in. It's sometimes impossible to believe that love is real when you are experiencing sadness in your life. Many relationships are breaking down and divorce is prevalent. Now is the time to take action if you want to heal an unhealthy relationship. It's time to get serious and clear out past partners from your chakra system so you can let love in again, this time, with the purity and sacredness that love deserves. We are not born to suffer. We are born to live amazing lives in our extraordinary beautiful world. Remember, it's the small things that matter in love. Go the extra mile, make the extra effort, communicate and stay when you feel like running away. Face difficulties and situations head on, up-front and centre. Fear and stress are our greatest obstacles, in love and in life.

At first, it can be overwhelming to feel this degree of love contained in the Divine Union Relationship. It is overwhelming to be loved unconditionally because there is no place to hide. It can feel quite foreign initially. Be patient, build a strong foundation of friendship and breathe and take it slowly. Divine love is our birthright, it's our gift. Please treat it with the respect and honour it deserves.

If you are looking for your Divine Union Relationship, know that you are about to begin the journey of a lifetime. It will lead you to an ultimate destination, a life filled with love, joy and wonderment that you won't believe is possible. But it is possible, it is real. The best way to give service is to pay it forward. Explore and experience the beauty and joy contained in your Divine Union. You can have it all!

Love Divine

A beautiful man walks to her side
He's reached out across the tide
Destiny now heralds the call
They both feel so enthralled
He has travelled to many lands
He looks across, the sea expands
And he wonders, where are you?
"I am here my love," she calls him to
The inner sanctum of her heart
To the magic divine love will impart
Sunshine shimmers upon the sea
He remembers her, she remembers he
The heart now opens to the sound
It's divinity that they have found
Tears of joy fill her eyes
They are finally together, she's so surprised
For it is he, her love divine
He's arrived through the hourglass of time

The look of love here so pure
Her light cascades beauty for sure
The essence of this light aflame
Re-unites these two who hold one name
The flame explodes and ignites with a roar
The essence of the sacred soars
Into the arms of divine grace
Gently now he touches her face
Eternity's rapture is transfixed to see
She has waited just for he
Love abounds on golden sighs
They never have to say goodbye
So much they want to share you see
This couple of true divinity
The purity of love is theirs to keep
Their love is accessed from the deep
Sacred energy fills the air
To herald this love beyond compare
He looks deeply into her eyes
He sighs, and places his hands on her side
The secrets and life's lessons you see
Sit between them and eternity
Illusions hold those who are blind
Time can erase the ties that bind
Like an eagle soaring now they are free
To play in life's eternal sea
The seed-atom unites these two
The earth is the playground they pursue
They are one, they share one view
Nothing can ever separate these two
Harps the music of the spheres
She hears this sound when he is near

As he adoringly looks into her soul
He sees she has experienced earthly woe
She waited for him, she always believed
That he would find the clues she left for he
Her heart knows it belongs to him
Only for him does her pure heart sing
Embrace this gift, this sacred key
That opens the door to divinity
Love is found in the sacred heart
These secrets of love we have impart
The Divine Union and its sacred clues
Will open a portal just for you
And when divine love finds its throne
You've finally found your sacred home

About the Omega Connection™

The principle of the Omega Connection™ offers education and practical techniques regarding the Divine Union Relationship. The current shift in consciousness will enhance our ability to accept new information that is being presented at this time. As we move forward with an open mind, we are being encouraged to explore the unfolding dynamics of love.

Most people are unaware that The Divine Union Relationship exists. It is unique in its ability to connect couples at the level of the soul which creates a deeper and more meaningful life. The flow on effect of subtle energy systems showcases the progress we need to take the next evolutionary steps.

The idea of the soul is a new concept to many people. It has been buried and forgotten in ancient teachings that are carved in the fabric of past civilisations. As the family of humanity, we are now ready to embrace our ancient past and modernise the wisdom teachings that history's footsteps have revealed.

For so long, we have been sitting on the edge of a known reality. Evolution won't ask us to repeat the same limitations of the past. The Omega Connection™ encourages an inquisitive curiosity; an openness to learn new ideas about the Divine Union Relationship. Be fearless and embrace the unknown and release the old ways of being. To this end, a new perspective and greater expansion occurs.

The word Omega means final. The Divine Union Relationship is a human relationship between two people that is revealed at the highest level we can attain and experience while incarnated in human form.

The greatest reason and soul purpose to strive for while living on planet Earth is to love and to be loved. Your soul is the portal to the sacredness of this journey. Beneath the pain and struggles the heart and soul has endured lies the purity of the Omega Connection™. It is the final and ultimate attainment of the soul's journey home.

Printed in the United States
By Bookmasters